Teacher Resource Book

Grade 2

Orlando Austin New York San Diego Toronto London

Visit *The Learning Site!*
www.harcourtschool.com

Printed in the United States of America

ISBN 0-15-339497-8

1 2 3 4 5 6 7 8 9 10 073 10 09 08 07 06 05 04

Contents

Vocabulary Activities

At the beginning of the year, you may want to have children begin an Art Vocabulary Log. Have children add unit vocabulary words as they learn them and include sketches and notes to help them remember what the words mean. Encourage children to list the words in alphabetical order, leaving space between entries for additional words.

Vocabulary word cards can be found on pages 7–22. These are the same vocabulary words that are in the *Student Edition.* Duplicate and distribute the cards. You may want to have children store the cards in a self-seal baggy. They can add the meaning, an example sentence, or a sketch to each card to help them learn the words. Children can use them as flash cards to read and to quiz each other. The word cards can also be used in a variety of games.

Word Sorts

Open Sort An open sort can be used to determine children's familiarity with the unit vocabulary. Distribute copies of the vocabulary cards for a new unit. Have children cut out the cards and work with a partner to sort them into meaningful piles. Then ask children to explain why they sorted the words as they did. For example, some children might group *repetition* with *pattern,* explaining that a pattern is repeated. Others might place *repetition* with *rhythm,* explaining that a rhythm is repeated. There are no wrong answers with an open sort.

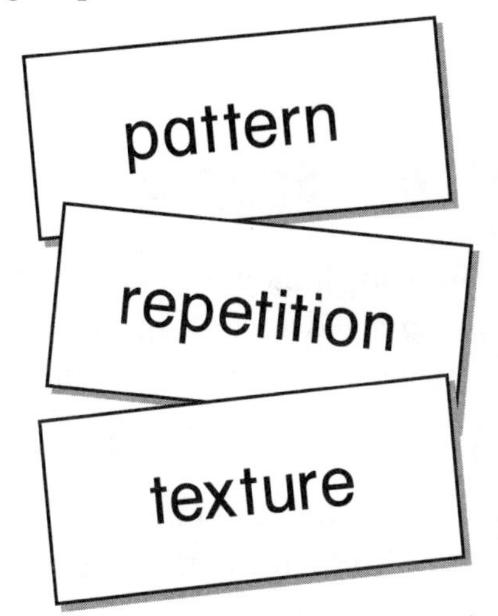

Closed Sort A closed sort can be used to determine children's understanding of the unit concepts. Distribute copies of the vocabulary cards at the end of a unit, and ask children to sort the words into specific categories. For example, display an *Art Print* and ask them to sort the words into two piles—one of words that relate to the artwork and one of words that do not.

Word Lists

At the beginning of a unit, write selected vocabulary words at the top of a chart. Throughout the unit, challenge children to add words that are related to each vocabulary word. At the end of the unit, each vocabulary word should have a list of related words that will help clarify its meaning.

RHYTHM	PATTERN	TEXTURE
beat	same	touch
tempo	over-and-over	bumpy
clap	repeat	smooth

Mystery Word

Invite a volunteer to come forward and face away from the group. Display a word card so that the remaining children can see it. Then cover the word card. Have the volunteer turn around and ask the group yes-or-no questions about the word until he or she can guess it.

Is it straight?

Is it an element?

True or False

Invite volunteers to use vocabulary words in true and false sentences. Have children give the thumbs-up signal if the sentence is true and a thumbs-down signal if the sentence is false. Examples of false statements: *An architect's job is to bake cakes. A landscape painting is a painting of a person.*

Word Square

To help children gain a thorough understanding of a particular art vocabulary word, have them make a word square. They begin by dividing a sheet of paper into four sections. Then ask them to do the following:

Section 1: Write the word.

Section 2: Write or draw something that represents the word.

Section 3: Write a definition of the word.

Section 4: Write or draw something that represents the word's opposite.

1	2
primary color	red yellow blue
3	**4**
one of the three basic colors from which all colors are made	orange purple green

Art Print Game

Display 6–8 *Art Prints*, or other images of artworks, around the classroom. Write vocabulary words on self-stick notes and distribute one to each child. (Some vocabulary words can be written more than once so that every child can participate.) Tell children to place their self-stick note on the area of an artwork that corresponds to their vocabulary word. Ask children to explain why they placed their notes where they did.

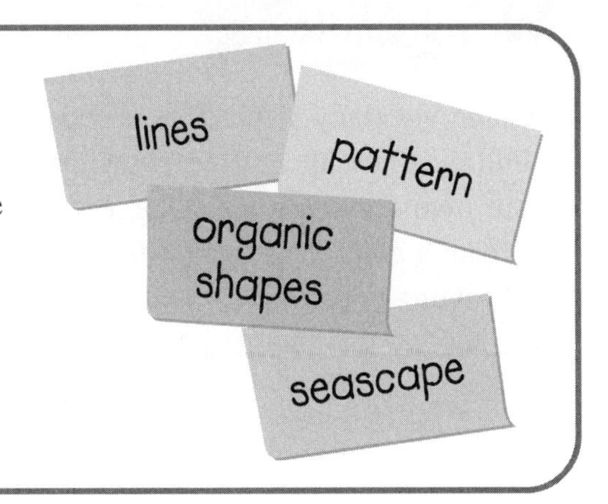

Name That Word

Display vocabulary word cards. Give children clues about a word, and call on volunteers to select and read aloud the appropriate word card. For example, say *I'm thinking of a word that means "marks that are straight or curved." (lines) I'm thinking of a word that means "a picture that some one draws of himself or herself." (self-portrait)*

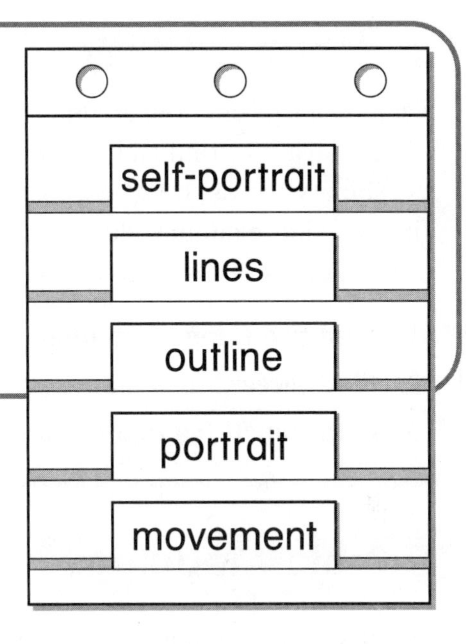

Describe It

Ask children to close their eyes and imagine an artwork that has certain qualities that you describe using vocabulary words. For example, say, *Imagine an artwork that has cool colors and a quiet mood. What does it look like?* A child might respond by saying *I see a painting of a pond early in the morning. The pond is blue, and there are green trees and plants all around it.*

Word Collage

Assign vocabulary words to groups or pairs of children. Have them glue magazine pictures and their own drawings onto a large sheet of paper to form a collage of images that relate to their word.

Scavenger Hunt

Send teams of children around the classroom or schoolyard to find and list items related to vocabulary words. Invite each team to share its findings. For example, children might be given a list like this of things to locate:

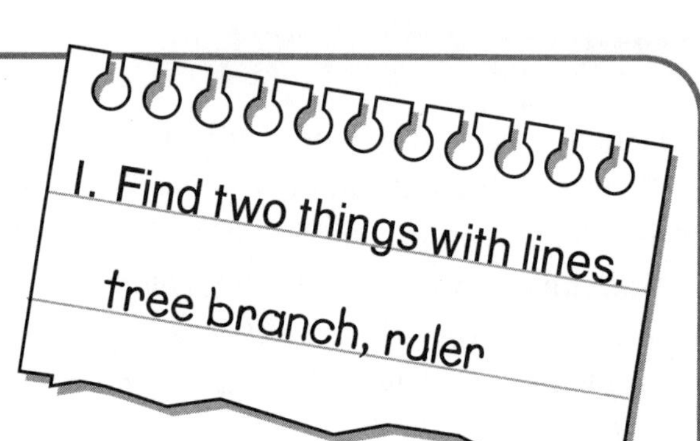

1. **Find two things with lines.**
2. **Find three things that are geometric shapes.**
3. **Find something that has an outline.**

Double Meanings

Discuss with children that many words used to talk about art have a slightly different meaning when used to talk about things like events or people. Distribute a set of vocabulary cards to each child. Then arrange children in pairs. Tell them to choose vocabulary words that have more than one meaning such as the word *value*. Have one child write a sentence using the word as it relates to art. The other should write a sentence using the word in another way. Tell children to draw a picture to illustrate their sentence. Then invite partners to share their work with the group.

value

The value of the color is very light.

value

The value of this car is very high.

Unit 1: Vocabulary Cards

free-form shapes

organic shapes

portrait

self-portrait

lines

outline

movement

geometric shapes

Unidad 1: Tarjetas con palabras del vocabulario

figuras de forma libre

figuras orgánicas

retrato

autorretrato

líneas

contorno

movimiento

figuras geométricas

Unit 2: Vocabulary Cards

value

tint

shade

mood

primary colors

secondary colors

warm colors

cool colors

Unidad 2: Tarjetas con palabras del vocabulario

Unit 2: Vocabulary Cards

seascape

horizon line

vista marina

línea del horizonte

Unit 3: Vocabulary Cards

texture

weaving

visual texture

pattern

repetition

print

rhythm

Unidad 3: Tarjetas con palabras del vocabulario

Unit 4: Vocabulary Cards

architecture	architect	landscape	foreground
form	sculpture	space	relief sculpture

arquitectura

arquitecto

paisaje

primer plano

forma

escultura

espacio

escultura en relieve

Unit 4: Vocabulary Cards

background

Unidad 4: Tarjetas con palabras del vocabulario

fondo

Unit 5: Vocabulary Cards

contrast

textiles

designs

emphasis

subject

balance

symmetry

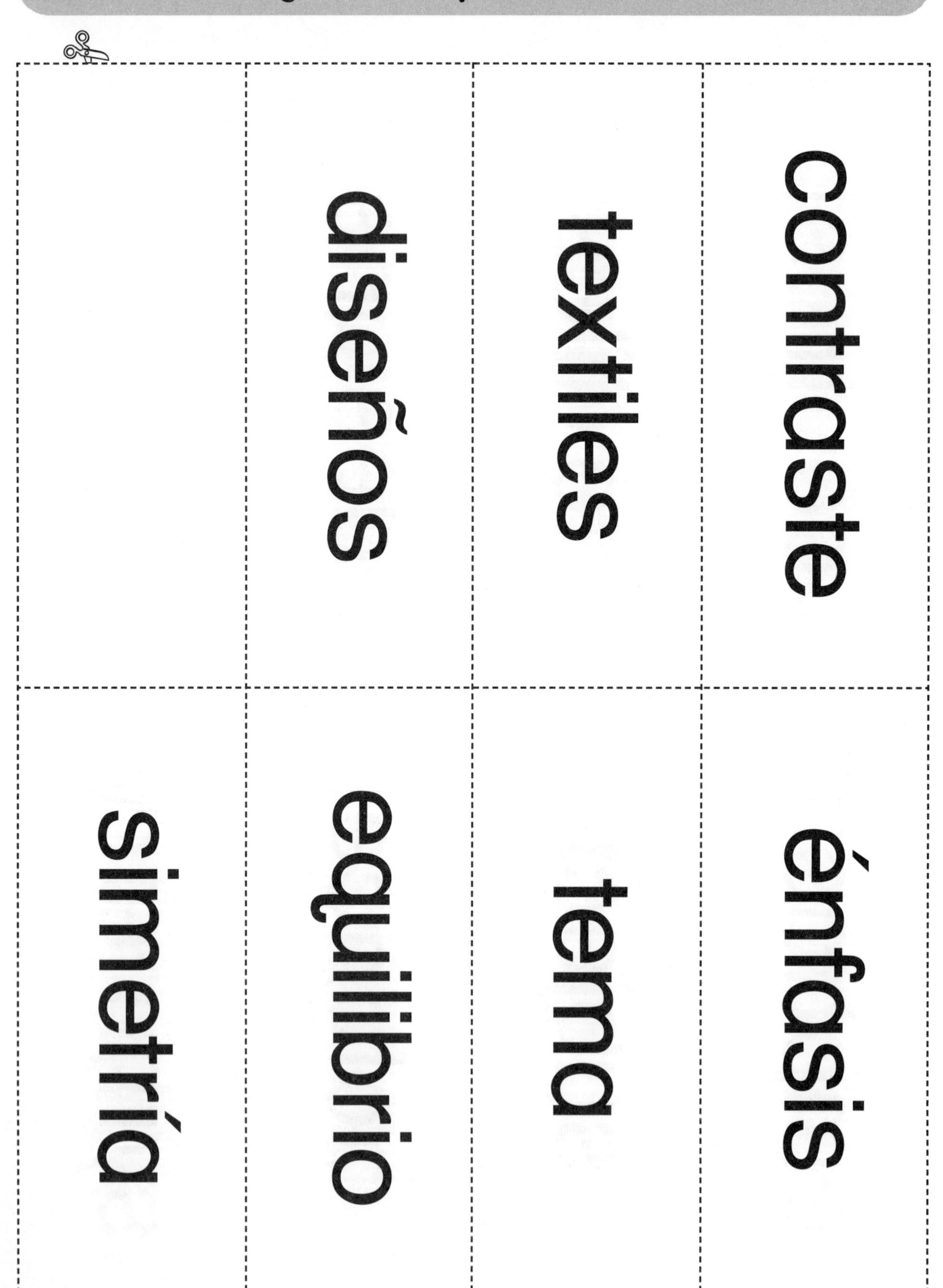
contraste
textiles
diseños
énfasis
tema
equilibrio
simetría

Unit 6: Vocabulary Cards

variety

story cloth

graphic art

mosaic

unity

symbol

still life

Unidad 6: Tarjetas con palabras del vocabulario

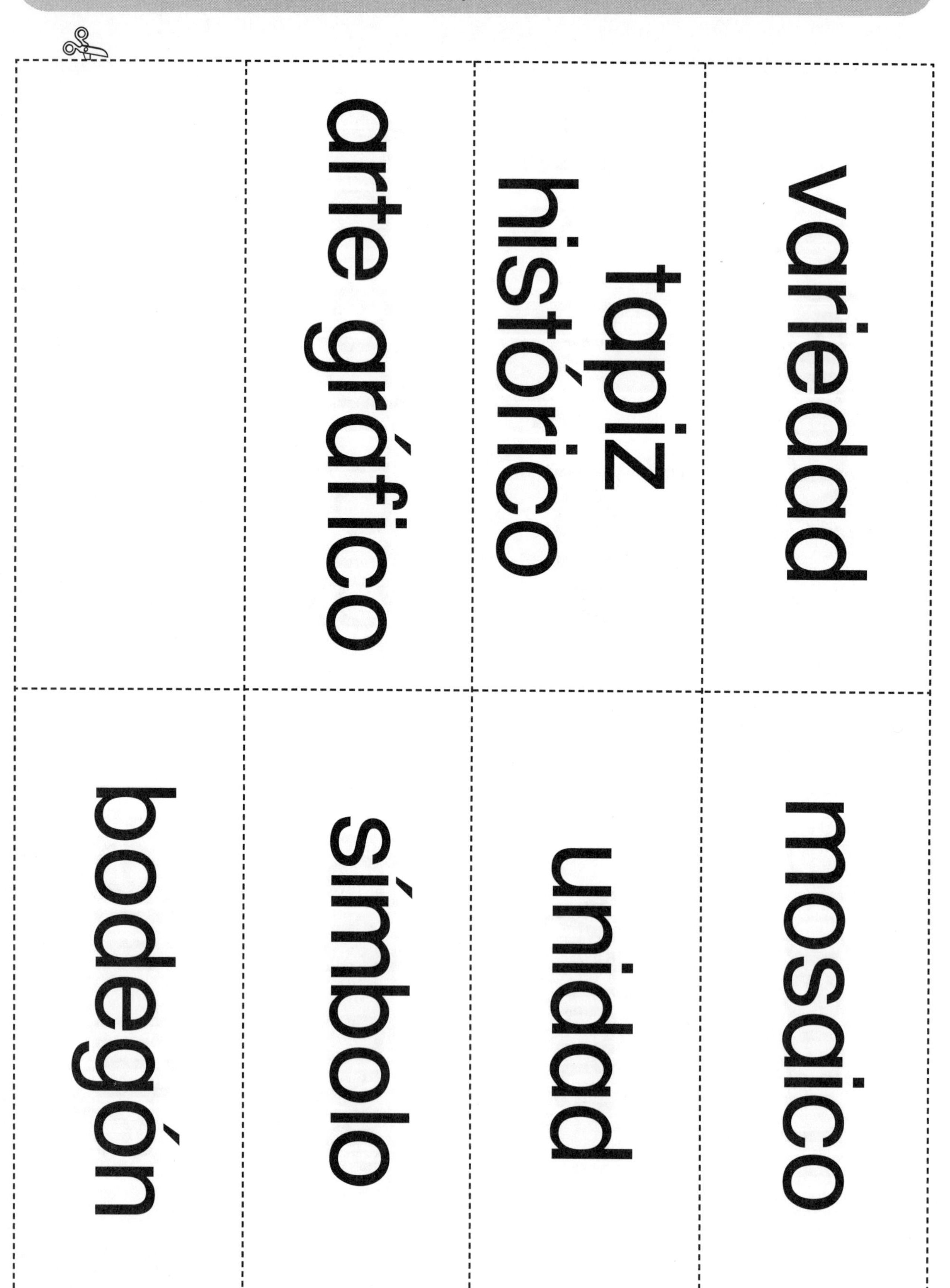

Reading Skill Card I

Make Inferences

What I See and Read +	What I Know =	What I Think

Reading Skill Card 2

Story Elements

Beginning

Characters:

Setting:

What is the problem?

Middle

What do the characters do about the problem?

Ending

How is the problem solved?

Focus Skill

Reading Skill Card 3

Important Details

Detail

Detail

Detail

This picture is about:

Detail

Detail

Detail

Compare and Contrast

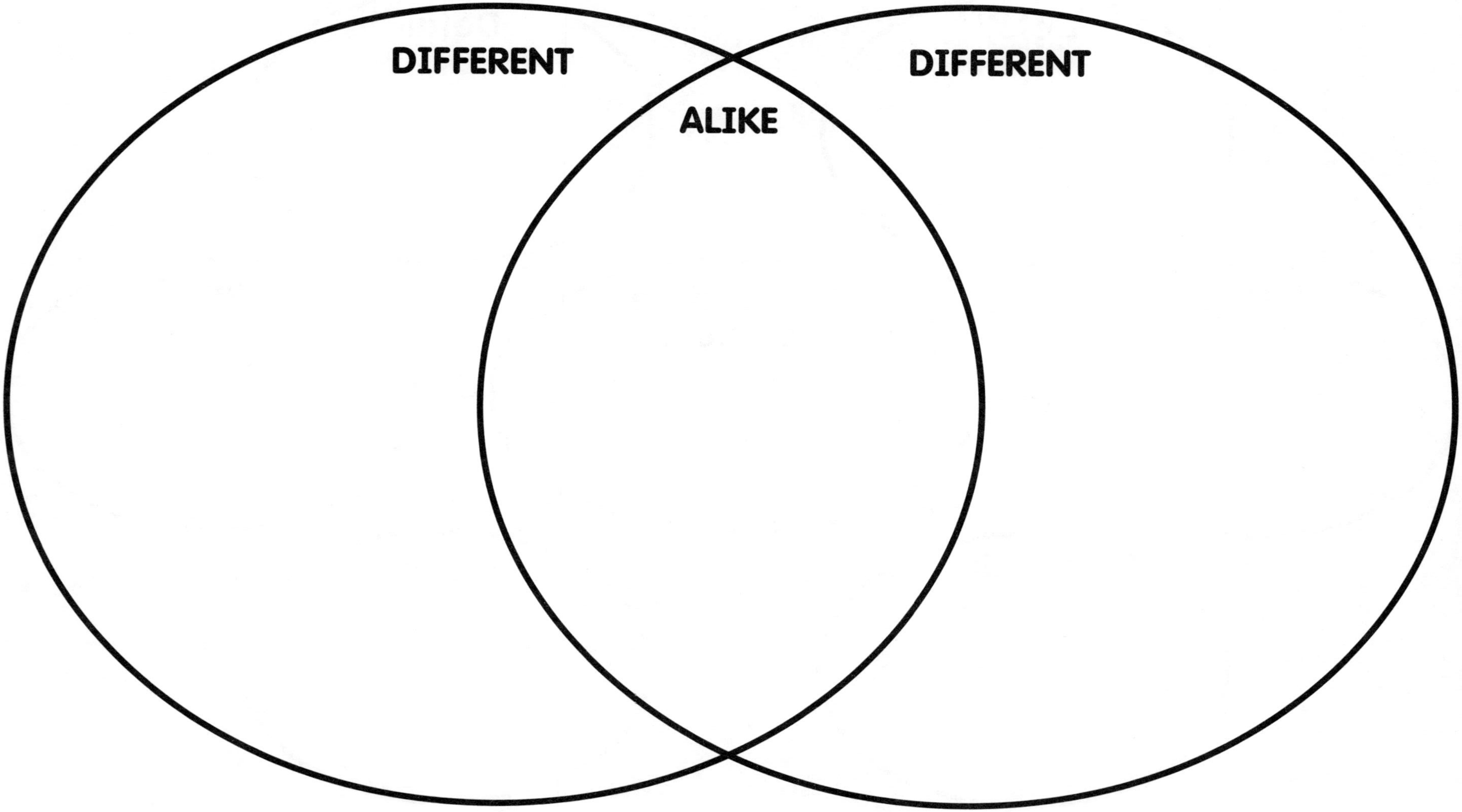

DIFFERENT

ALIKE

DIFFERENT

Reading Skill Card 5

Main Idea

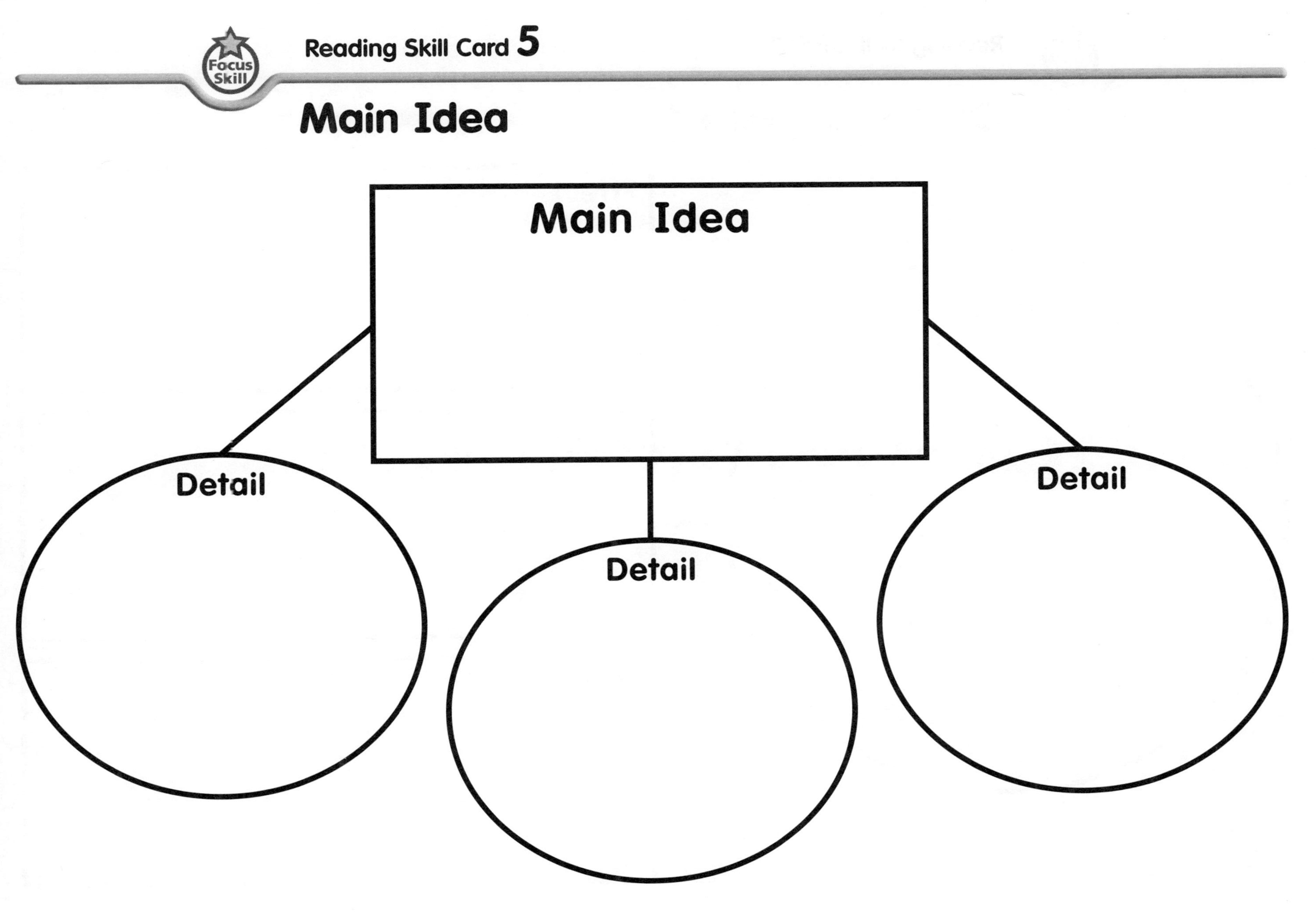

Focus Skill

Reading Skill Card 6

Cause and Effect

Cause

Effect

Effect

Effect

Idea Wheel—Spinner

To the teacher: You may wish to copy the spinner onto heavy paper and laminate it. Attach the arrow with a brad. Early finishers can spin the spinner and do the corresponding activity from page 30. The spinner may also be used for other games and activities.

Idea Wheel—Activities

1. Cut out a picture from a magazine. Cut it in half. Glue one half on a sheet of paper, and draw the other half.
2. Write your initials large. Add lines, shapes, and colors to make them look like objects.
3. Draw an interesting object you see in the classroom.
4. Cut colored paper into small shapes. Glue them onto paper. Make a pattern.
5. Draw a tree. Use only lines.
6. Create an artwork that shows how you feel.
7. Look at the patterns and designs on clothing. Copy one on a sheet of paper.
8. Draw a large bowl or plate. Decorate it with a design.
9. Find something that is very small. Draw it very large to fill a whole page.
10. Draw lightning or a night scene on dark paper. Use white chalk or a white crayon.

1. Build something with recyclables or scraps. Glue or tape it together.
2. Cut out paper shapes. Glue them to form a picture.
3. Look closely at your face in a mirror. Draw yourself.
4. Color a rainbow in your own style.
5. Arrange classroom objects in an interesting way. Draw the still life.
6. Make a frame for one of your artworks. Decorate it.
7. What things are shaped like a triangle? Draw them. Cut others from a magazine.
8. Trace your hand. Fill it with different lines and colors.
9. Fold paper in fourths. Rub with a crayon. Put a different texture in each part.
10. Roll clay into shapes. Make an animal or a person.

To the teacher: Use these activities for early finshers or for children to do during free time. Use with the spinner on page 29. Alternate the lists.

Art Display Card

What I liked about making this artwork:

Other things I want to tell about it:

fold

Artist's Name ______________________

Title of Artwork ______________________

____

Date ______________________

How I made my artwork: ______________________

____

____

Color Wheel

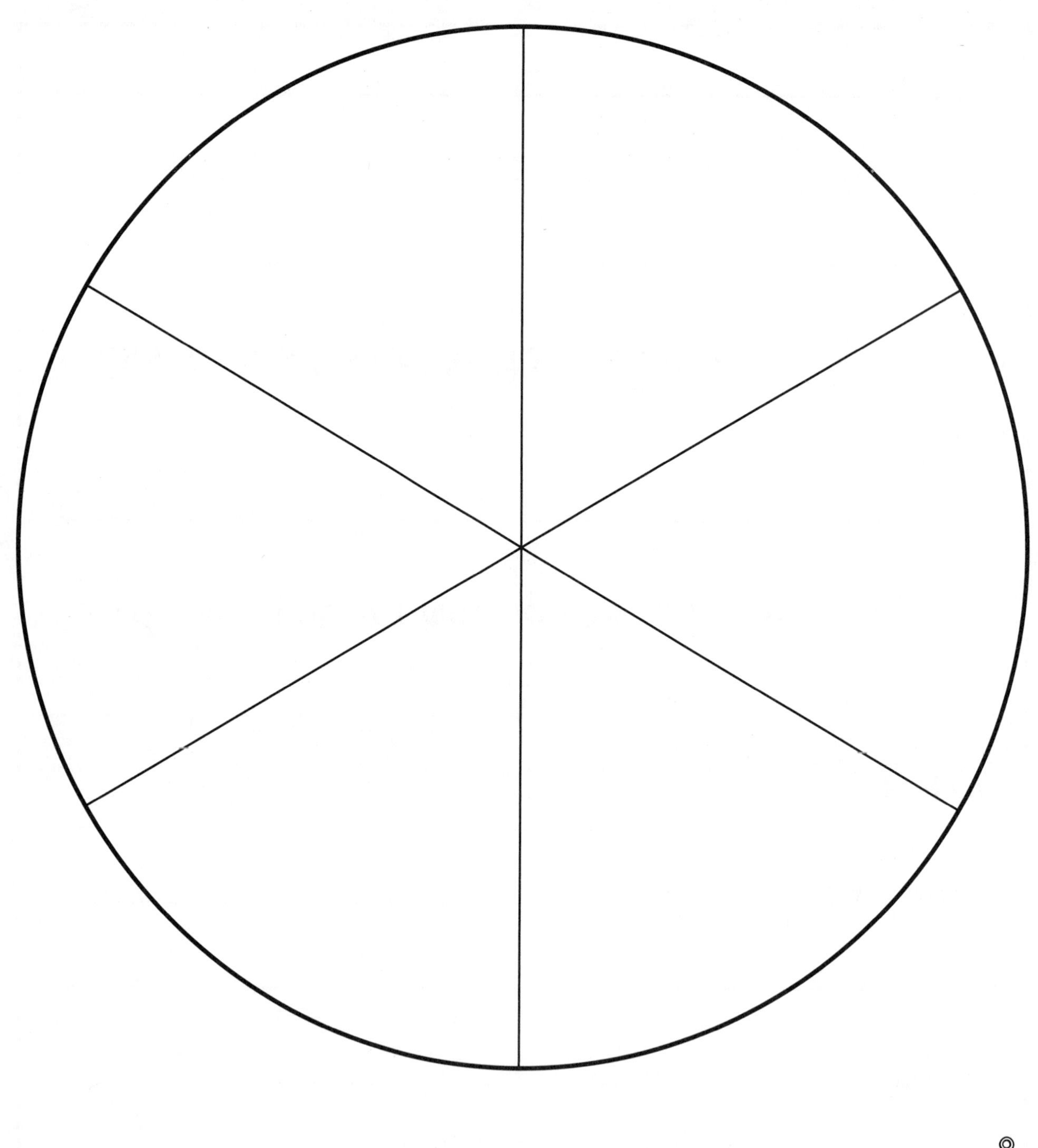

red	orange	yellow	green	blue	violet

To the teacher: Have children color or paint each section of the color wheel. Then have them cut out and glue on the color word labels.

Your Passport to Art

You can travel around the world through art, but first you need a passport. Cut out this page and fold it. On the lines and on the inside, list artworks you learn about. Happy travels!

Fold

Draw or glue your picture here.

Name____________________

Artwork	Location

Let the love of
ART
take you places!

United States Map

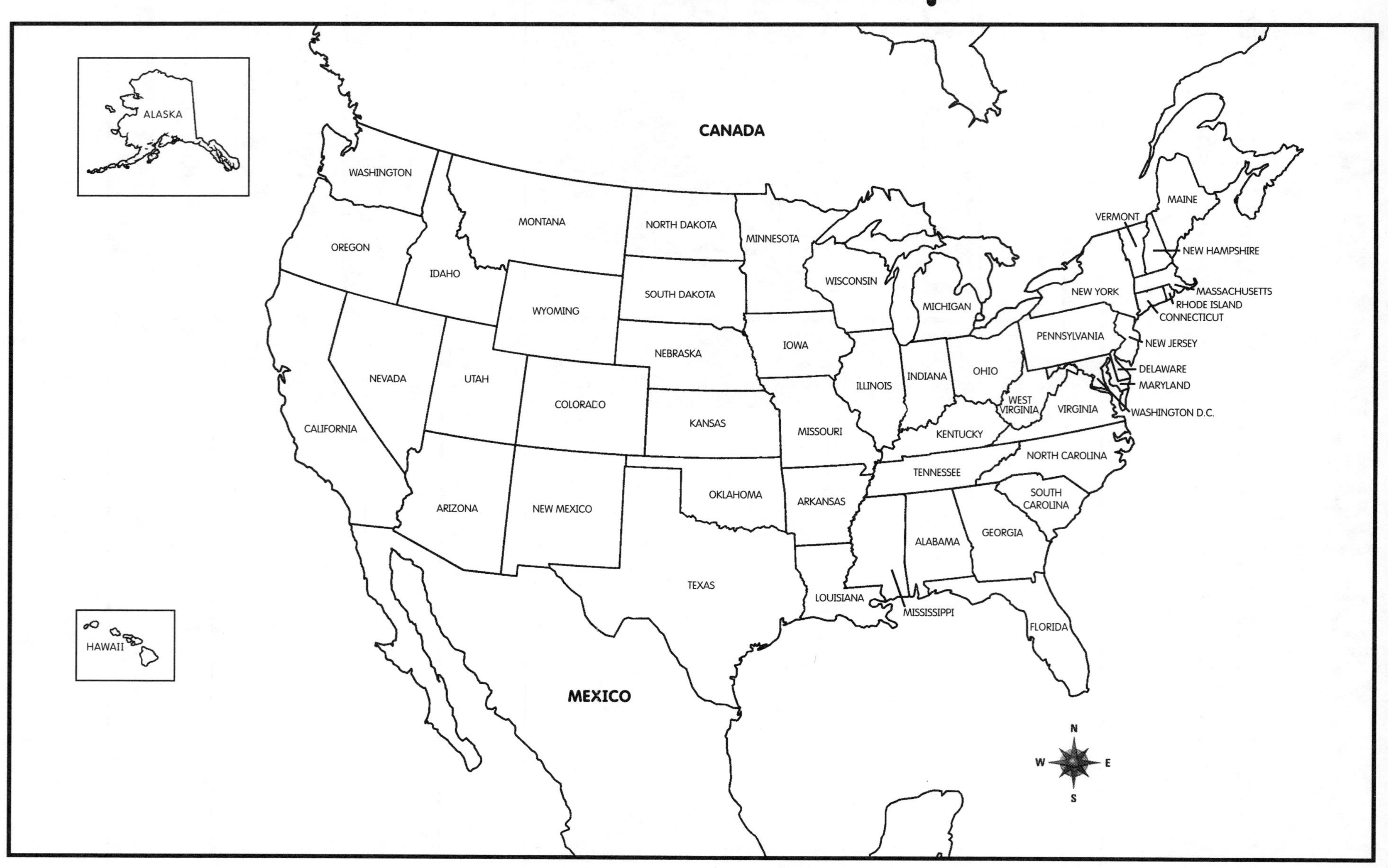

World Map

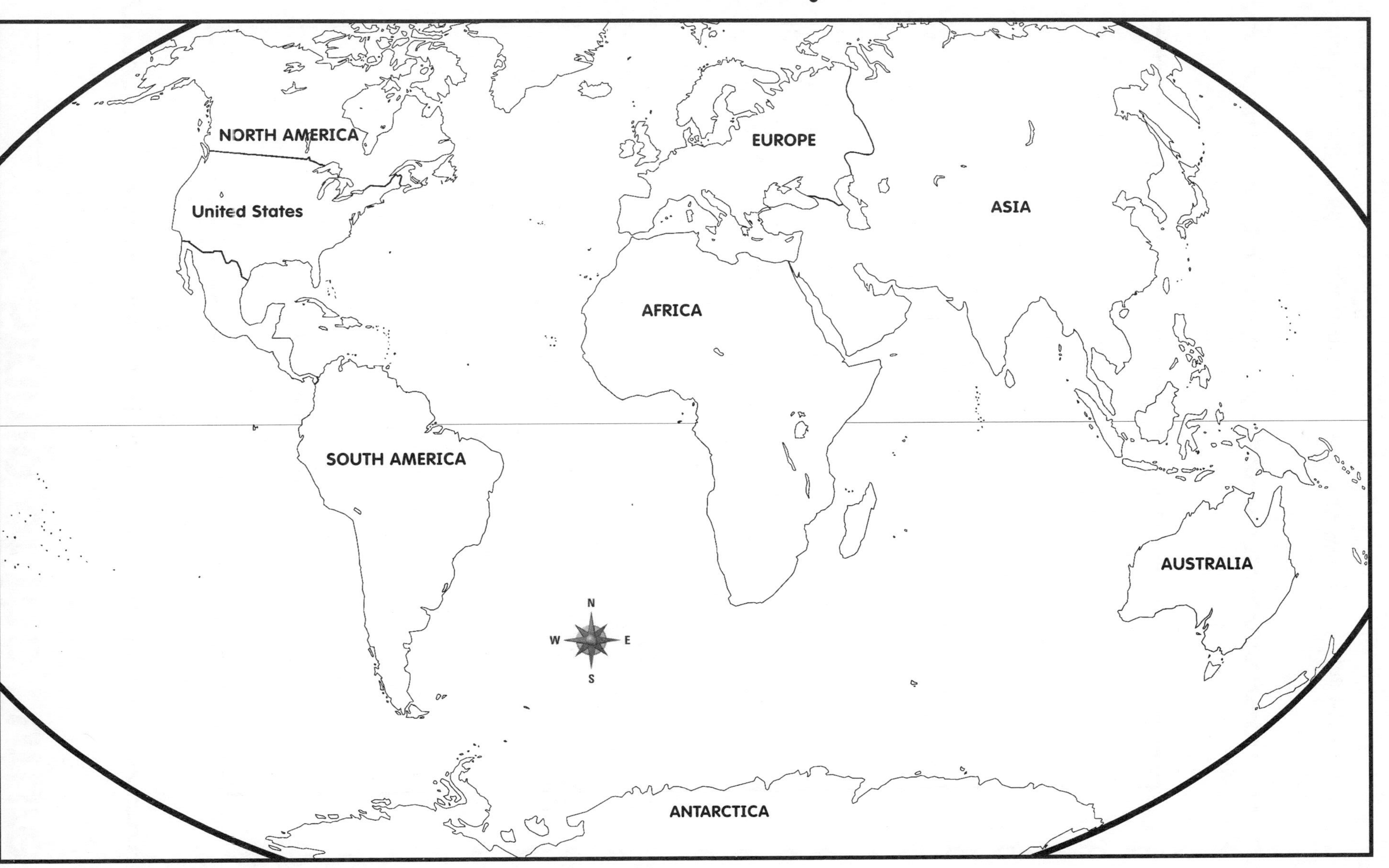
NORTH AMERICA
United States
EUROPE
ASIA
AFRICA
SOUTH AMERICA
AUSTRALIA
N
W
E
S
ANTARCTICA

____________'s Stamp of the Future

To the teacher: Use this for the Quick Activity for the Artist's Workshop Stamp of the Future project, *Teacher Edition* page 139.

Pyramid Pattern

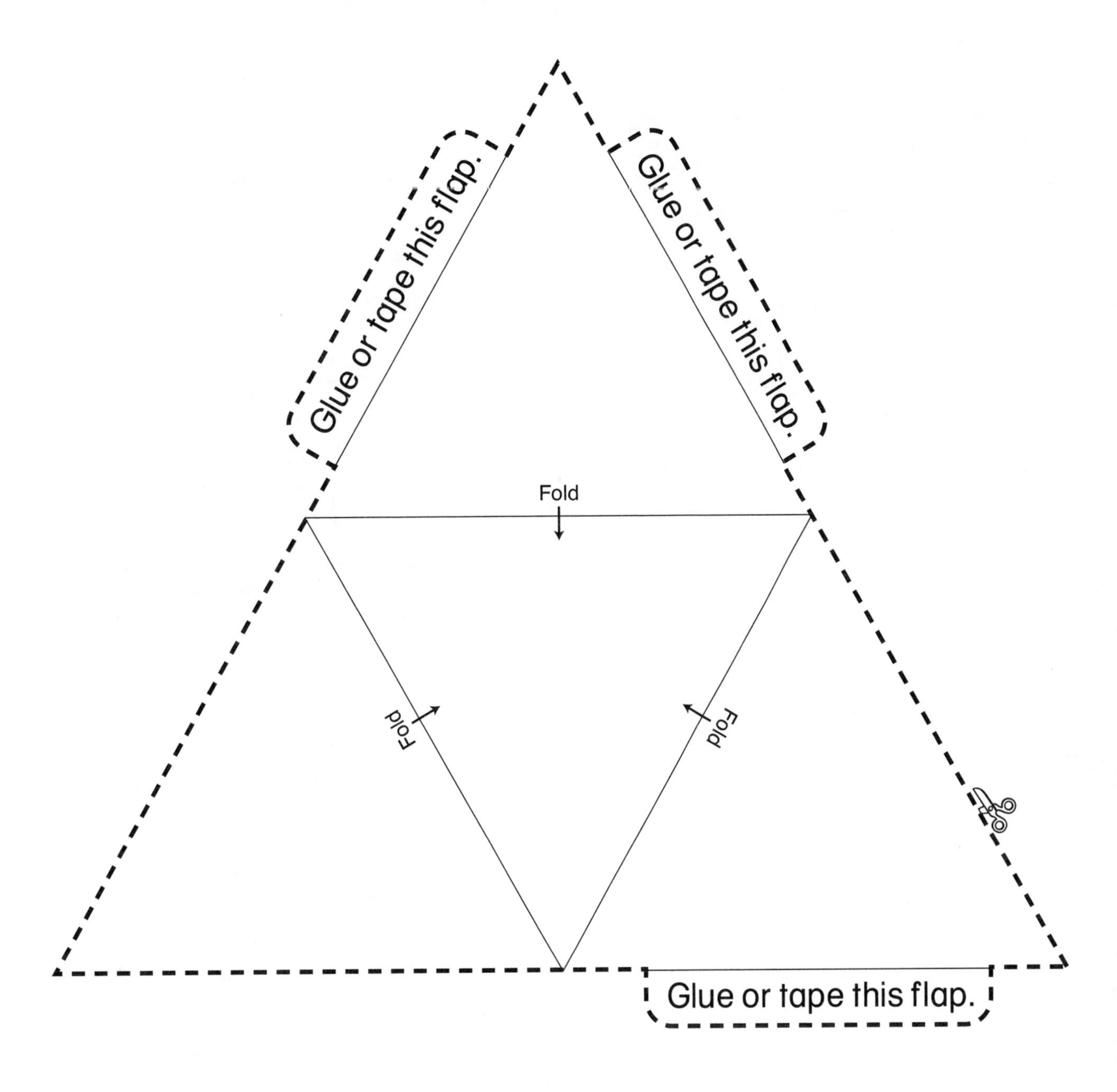

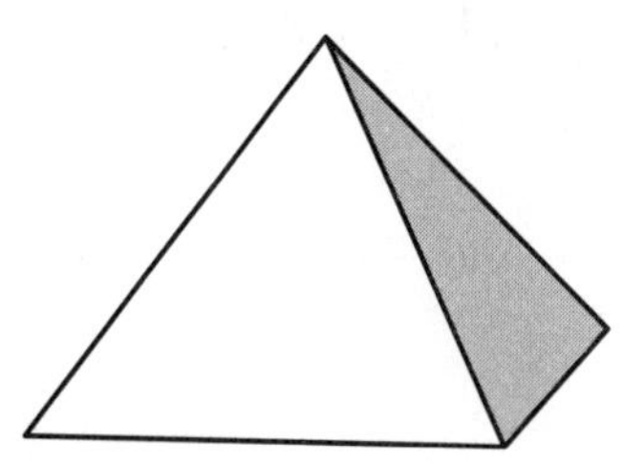

To the teacher: Have children cut out the pattern, leaving on the flaps. Next they turn over the pyramid and color or decorate the blank side. This will be the outside. Then have children fold and assemble the pyramid, providing help as needed. Children can use this pattern when learning about Egyptian art and about form and space.

Near and Far Pictures

To the teacher: Have children cut out the pictures and arrange them on a landscape they create. Remind them that things in the foreground often seem to be larger than things in the background. Artists often place larger things in the foreground to create a sense of depth and distance. Encourage children to add to their landscapes.

Make a Pinwheel

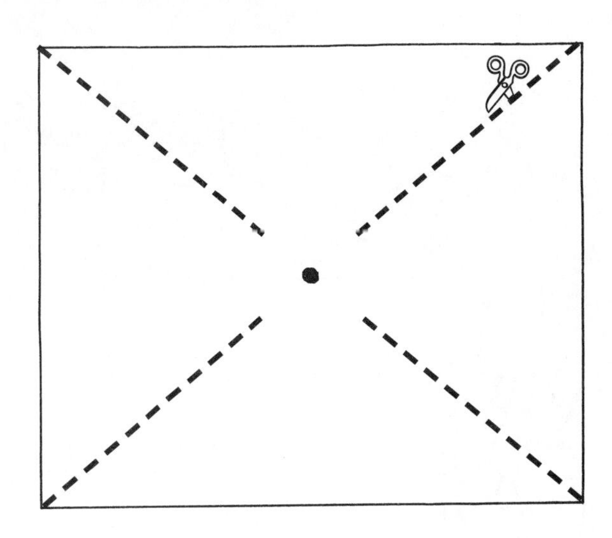

1. Cut along the dashed lines.

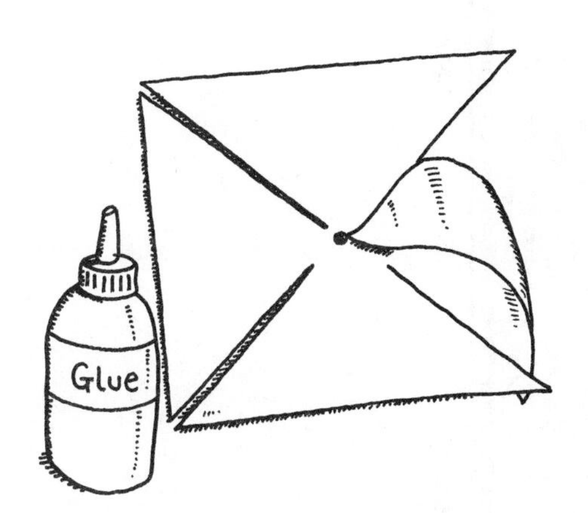

2. Glue the left tip of one triangle to the center.
3. Do the same with all the triangles.

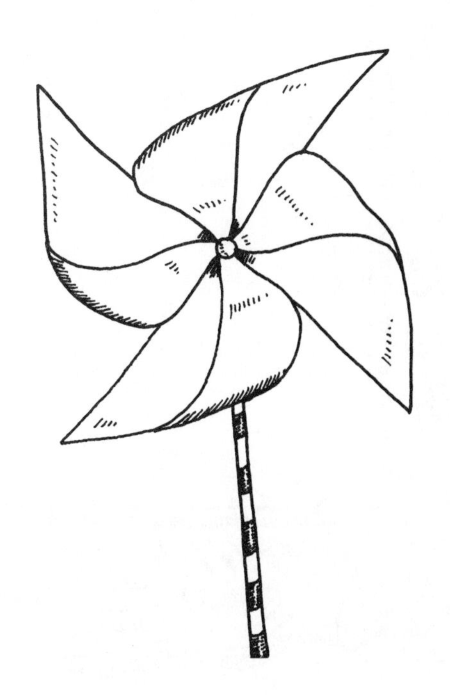

4. Put a brad through the center of the pinwheel.
5. Put the brad through a straw.

Fancy Frame

My Viewfinder

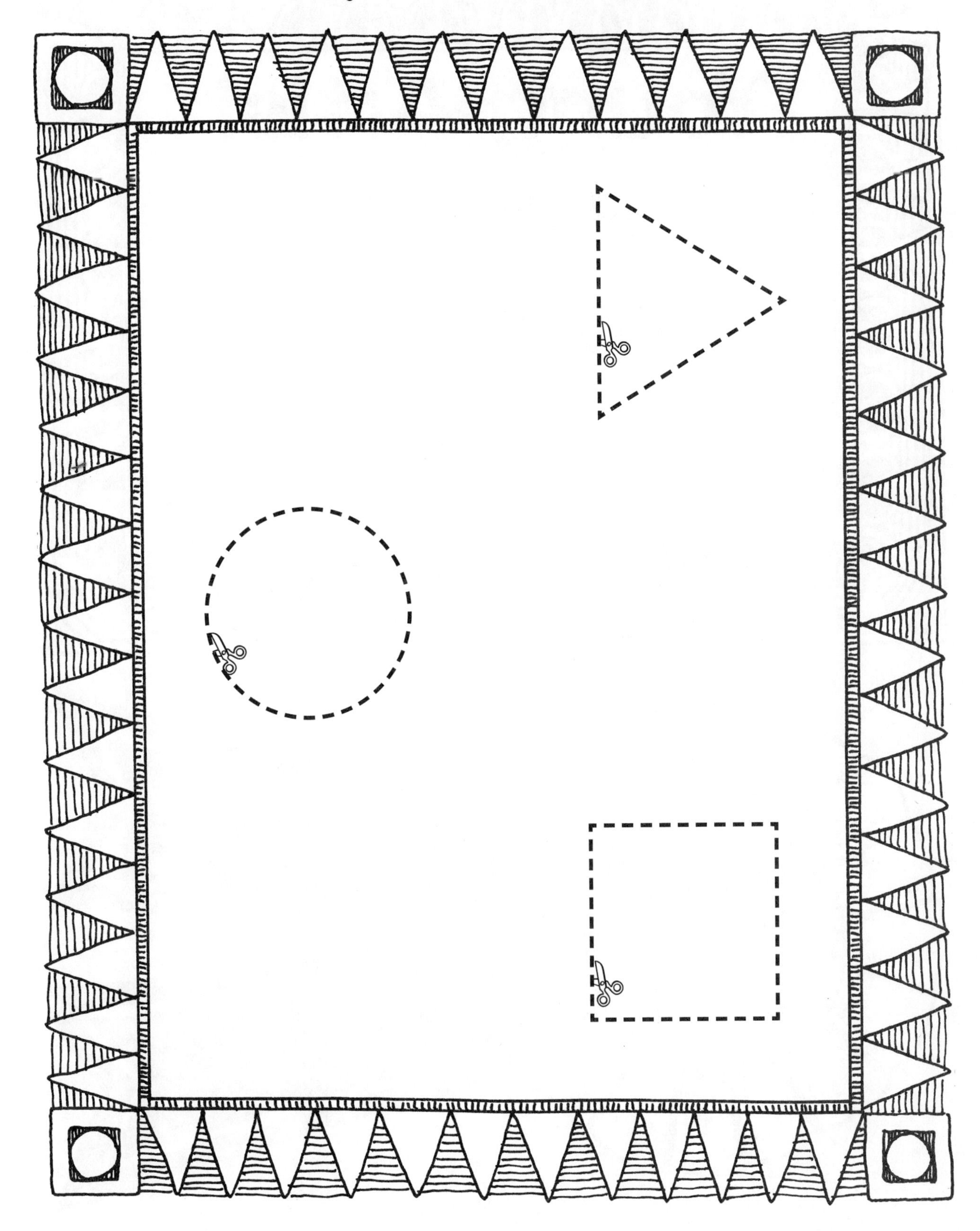

To the teacher: Have children cut out the center shapes and use the viewfinder to look through one opening at a time to focus on specific areas of an artwork.

Young Artist Award

Congratulations

______________________________!

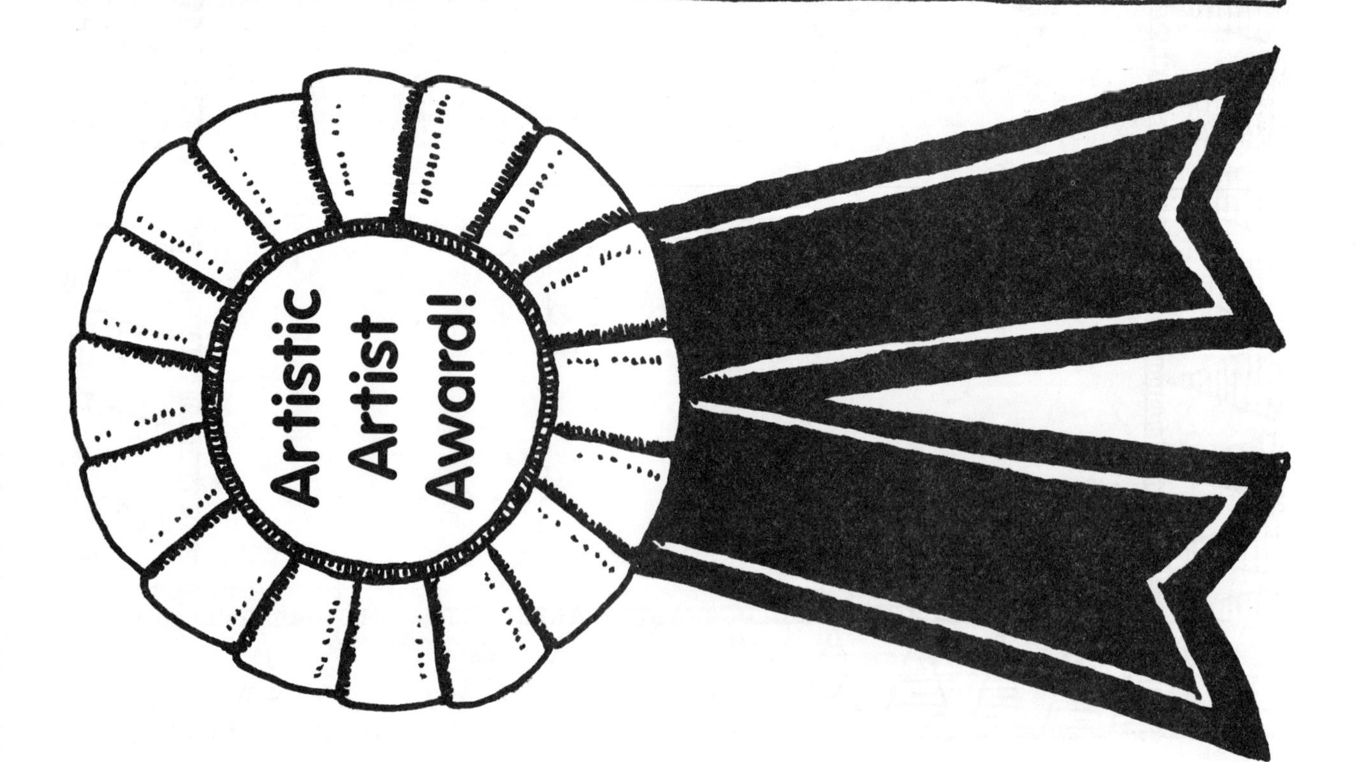

Name ______________________________

Tree Scene

MATERIALS

- construction and tissue paper
- pencil
- scissors
- glue
- crayons, markers

Plan

Think of a place where there are trees.

Create

1. Draw the place. Outline the trees.

2. Use many kinds of lines to make the tree bark look real.

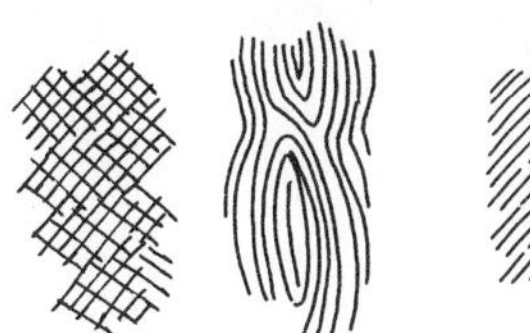

3. Add paper leaves.

Reflect

What kinds of lines did you use? How would the bark feel if you could touch it?

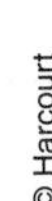

Name ____________________

Cartoon Story

MATERIALS

- drawing paper
- crayons, markers, or colored pencils

Plan

Think of a story that has cartoon characters moving, like running or jumping.

Create

1. Fold a sheet of paper two times.

2. Draw a part of the cartoon story in each section.

3. Use lines to show things moving.

4. Add words to tell the story. Then write about the kinds of lines you used to show movement.

Reflect

How do the lines help tell your story?

Name ______________________________

Abstract Collage

MATERIALS

- construction paper
- scissors
- glue
- yarn or string

Plan

Think of ways to put geometric shapes together to make other shapes.

Create

1. Cut out geometric shapes like circles, ovals, squares, and triangles.

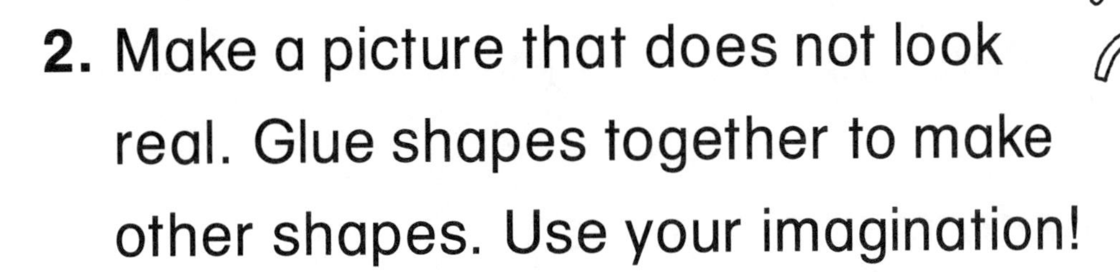

2. Make a picture that does not look real. Glue shapes together to make other shapes. Use your imagination!

3. Glue on yarn to add interesting lines.

Reflect

What geometric shapes did you use? What message or ideas do you see in your artwork?

Name ________________________________

Matisse Collage

MATERIALS

- scrap paper, wallpaper, wrapping paper
- scissors
- glue
- construction paper

Plan

Think about a scene with plants and animals. It could be on a farm, under the sea, or even around your own home.

Create

1. Make the scene. Cut out shapes like Henri Matisse did in his art on *Student Edition* page 34.

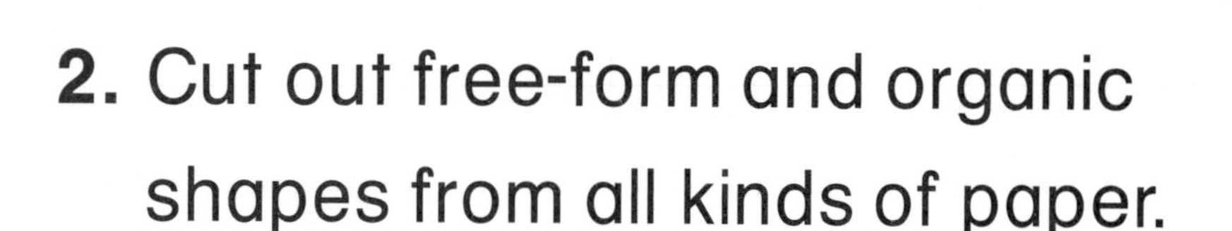

2. Cut out free-form and organic shapes from all kinds of paper.

3. Glue the shapes onto paper.

Reflect

What is the most interesting shape you made? Why do you think so?

Name ____________________

Self-Portrait

MATERIALS

- unbreakable mirror
- paper
- tempera paints, watercolor crayons, brushes
- crayons, markers, chalk, oil pastels, or colored pencils

Plan

Look closely at your face in a mirror. Notice shapes like circles and ovals.

Create

1. Draw an oval for your face. Draw your eyes halfway down. Finish your face, hair, and body.

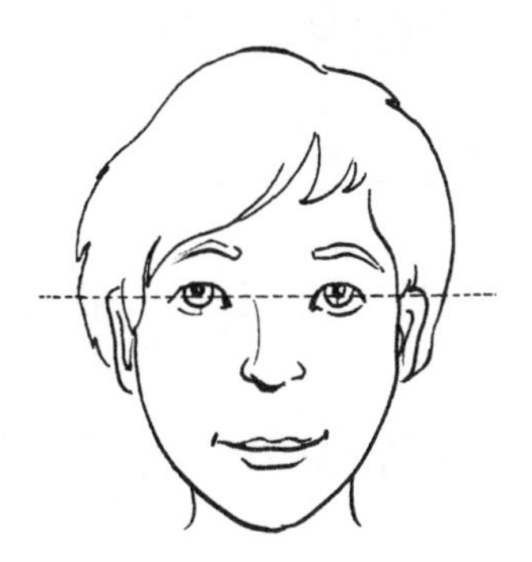

2. Add something that shows what you like to do.

3. Add color. Pick what will work best for your self-portrait, such as paint, crayons, or both.

Reflect

What did you learn by doing your self-portrait? What shapes did you use?

Name ______________________________

Mixing New Colors

MATERIALS

- white paper
- tempera paints (red, blue, yellow)
- paintbrushes
- paper plates

Plan

Think of how to create new colors by mixing colors.

Create

Primary Colors	Secondary Colors
red yellow blue	orange green violet

1. Mix a primary color with a secondary color that is next to it on the color wheel to make an **intermediate color**.
2. Mix colors that are across from each other, like red and green, to make brown or gray.
3. Experiment! Mix all kinds of colors.
4. Use your colors on a pinwheel as on *Student Edition* page 47 or to paint something else you choose.

Reflect

Which color do you like best? How did you make it?

Name ____________________

Sand Painting

MATERIALS

- sand
- powdered tempera paints
- jars
- pencils or straws
- spoons

Plan

Think of a design that has both warm colors and cool colors.

Create

1. Mix powdered paint with sand to make red, yellow, orange, blue, green, and violet.

2. Pour layers of sand into a jar. Use warm colors and cool colors in interesting ways.

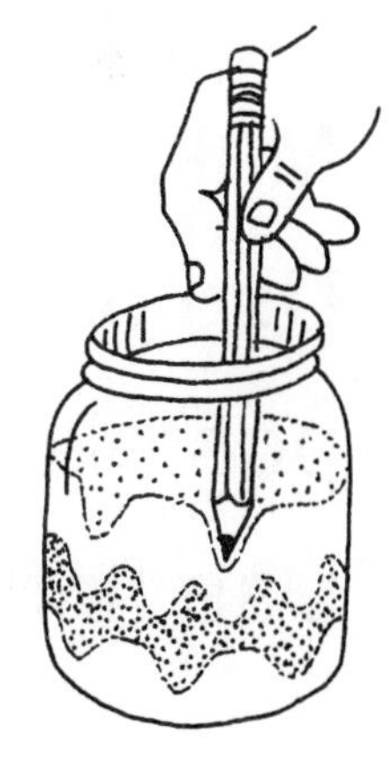

3. Poke down around the edges. Be creative! You can do this after each layer or when you are done.

Reflect

How do the colors in your art make you feel? Why?

Name ____

3-D Bouquet

MATERIALS

- simple, opaque vase
- paper
- tempera paints (red, yellow, blue, black, white)
- watercolor paints, chalk, oil pastels
- paintbrushes

Plan

Look at a real vase. Notice that some parts look light and some dark.

Create

1. Draw and paint a vase.
2. Use black to mix a shade of the color of your vase. Paint one side darker to make it look 3-D.
3. Make a bouquet of flowers. Use paint, chalk, or oil pastels. Mix colors. Use tints and shades.
4. Add a shadow.

Reflect

Where did you use tints and shades?

How did you make your bouquet look 3-D?

Mood Scenery

MATERIALS

- butcher paper
- construction paper
- oil pastels, chalk, paints, brushes
- scissors, glue
- craft sticks

Plan

Think of a story scene to create. What is the mood?

Create

1. Color or paint your story scene on large paper. Use color to help show the mood.
2. Cut out characters. Glue them onto craft sticks.
3. Hang up your scene. Shine a light. Put your puppets in front of the light so that their shadows are in your scene. Tell your story.

Reflect

What mood did you show? What colors did you use?

Name ______________________________

Fish Print Seascape

MATERIALS

- model fish or textured items
- white paper
- oil pastels, crayons, markers
- tempera paints
- paintbrushes

Plan

Think about a place with water, such as a lake or the ocean.

Create

1. Put paint on a model fish or an object with texture.

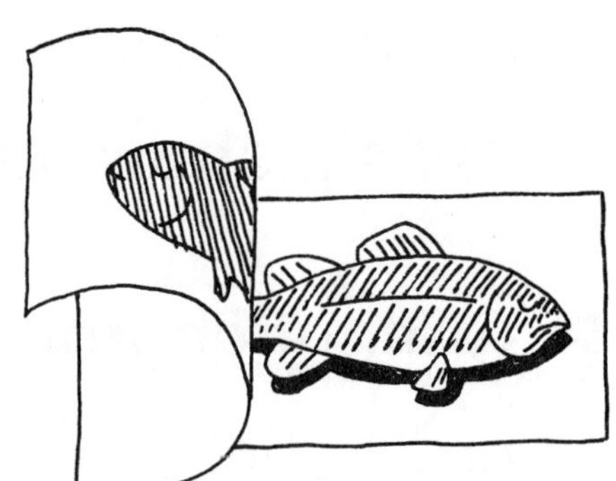

2. Lay a sheet of paper over the fish or object. Rub gently all over to make a print. Pull off the paper. If you used a textured object, cut out a fish shape.

3. Create a seascape with your fish in it. Color things in, on, and above the water.

Reflect

What is going on in your scene? What makes your artwork a seascape?

Name ________________________________

Picture Frame

MATERIALS

- 8" x 14" rectangle tracer
- 11" x 17" paper
- pencils, scissors
- markers, crayons, colored pencils, watercolor paints

Plan

Think of a design for a frame.

Create

1. Center the rectangle on the larger paper. Trace.

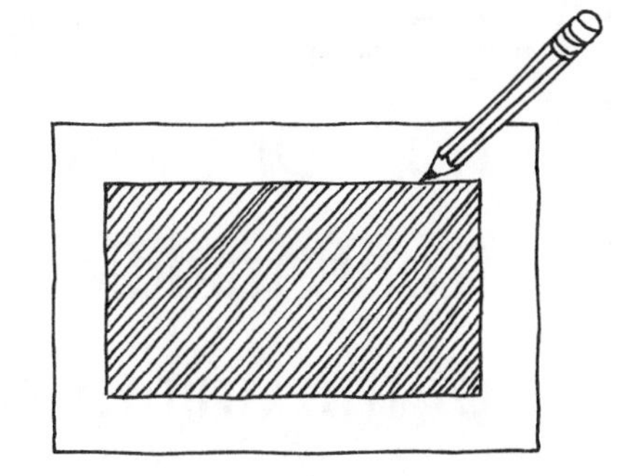

2. Fold the paper in half. Cut out the middle. Open it. Draw a design in pencil on one half. Press hard.

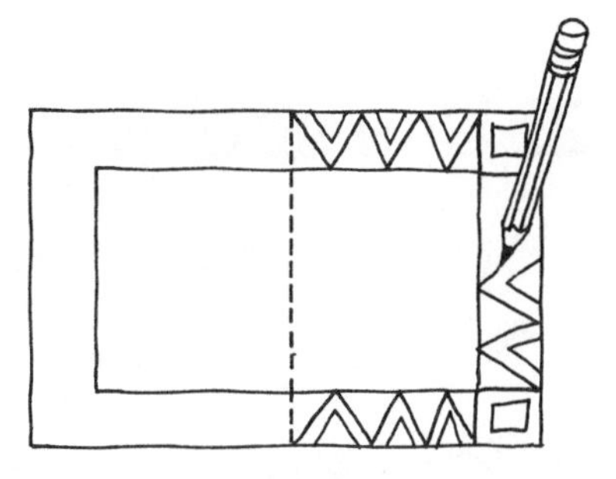

3. Fold the paper in half. Rub the design onto the other side. Outline with a marker and add color.

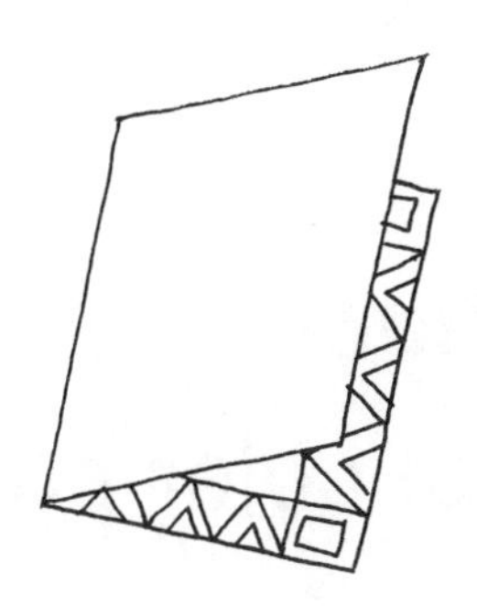

Reflect

What do you notice about the two halves of the frame?

Name ________________________________

Stand-up Art

MATERIALS

- construction paper
- scissors
- sponges or cardboard
- clothespins
- tempera paints
- glue

Plan

Think about the shape of an animal or object you like.

Create

1. Fold three sheets of paper in half. Draw and cut out the front, middle, and end parts of the animal or object. Don't cut along the fold.

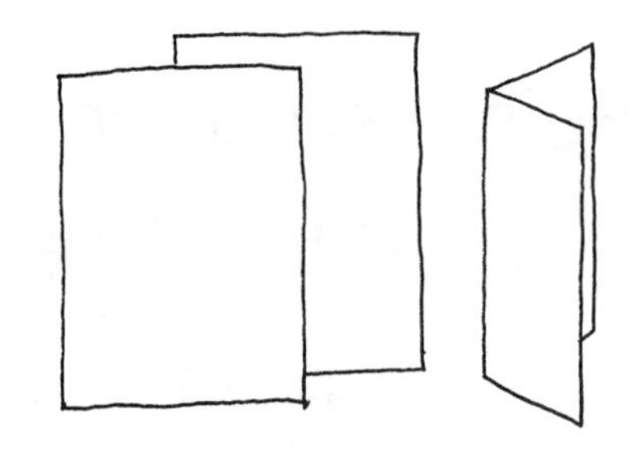

2. Use sponges to print a pattern of colors.

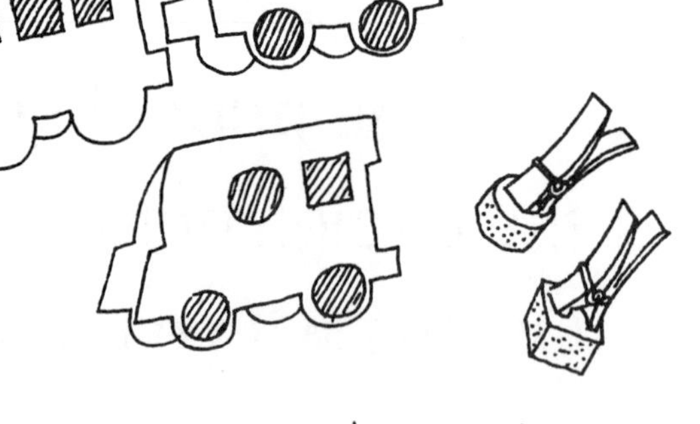

3. Glue paper strips to connect the parts.

Reflect

What color patterns did you make?

Name ____________________

Rhythm Near and Far

MATERIALS

- paper
- pencils
- watercolor or tempera paints
- paintbrushes

Plan

Imagine trees, plants, and animals you would see in a forest or jungle.

Create

1. Draw some trees in a row. Make each tree smaller than the one before it.

2. Add plants, animals, and other things to add to the rhythm.

Reflect

Which tree looks the closest to you? Which looks farthest away? What is the rhythm of your artwork?

Name ____________________________________

Twig Weaving

MATERIALS

- y-shaped twigs
- scissors
- yarn, string, paper, vines, ribbon, or raffia
- found objects like shells, seed pods, beads, buttons

Plan

Think about patterns and textures to put in a weaving.

Create

1. Tie one end of the yarn to the top of a branch. Wrap the yarn around two parts of it. Tie a knot at the bottom.

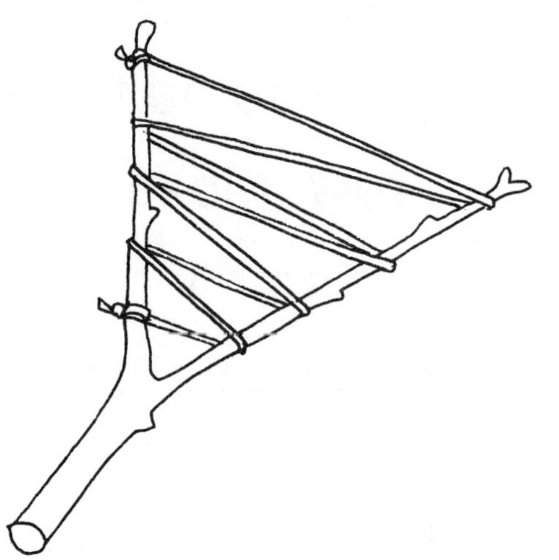

2. Weave over and under.

3. Put objects between the strands of the weaving or tie them on.

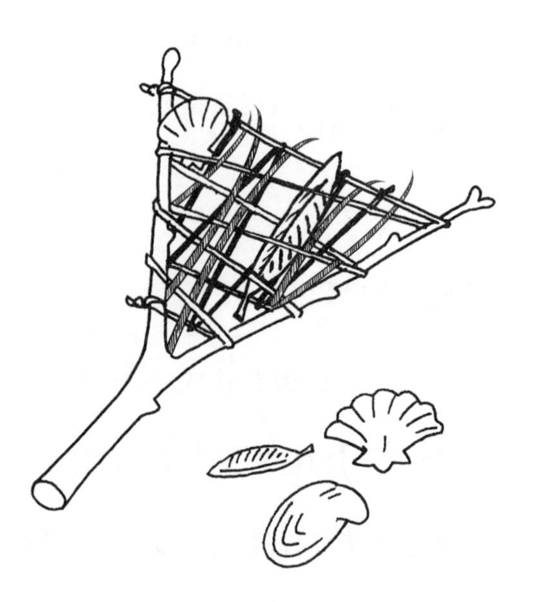

Reflect

What patterns and textures does your weaving have?

Name ______________________________

Animal Scratch Art

MATERIALS

- paper
- crayons
- liquid soap
- black tempera paint, brushes
- toothpicks or paper clips

Plan

Think about animals and the textures of their skin, fur, and other body coverings.

Create

1. Color a sheet of paper with bright colors. Press hard.

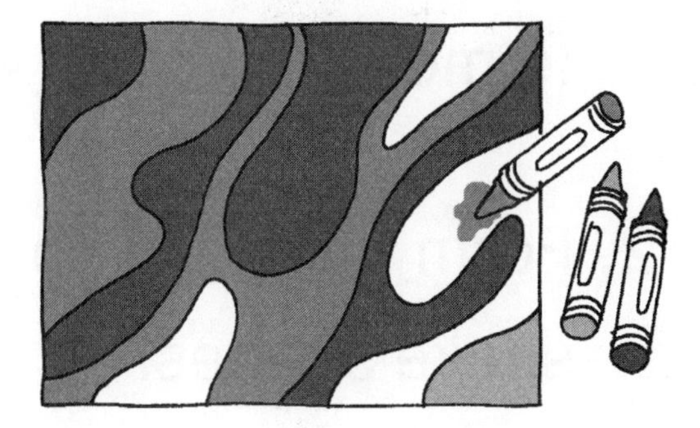

2. Add a little liquid soap to black paint. Paint the paper. Let it dry.

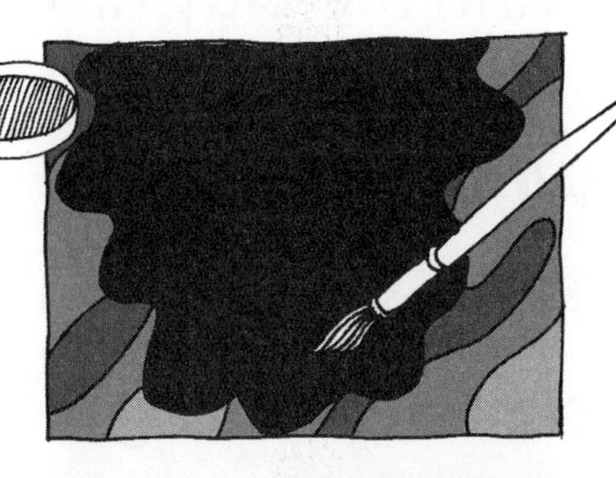

3. Scratch out an animal, showing its textures.

Reflect

What textures did you show? How did you make them?

Name ________________________________

Coil Pot

MATERIALS

- several colors of clay

Plan

Think about making a pot out of clay.

Create

1. Mix different colors of clay together to make the color you want.

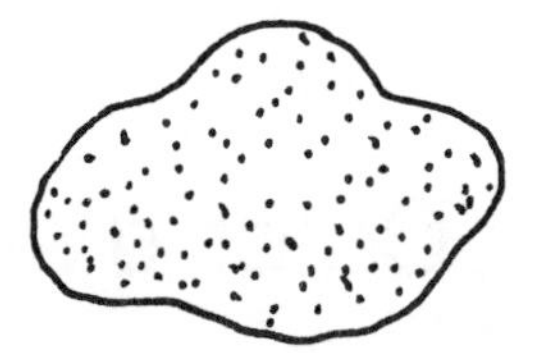

2. Form the clay into long snake shapes.

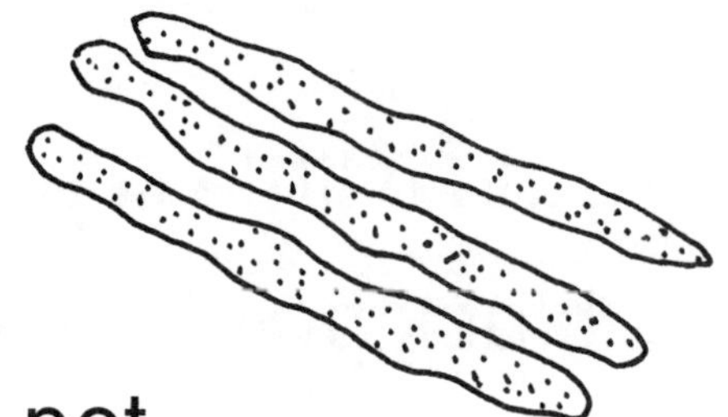

3. Wind the clay around to form a pot.

4. Write a fact about your clay pot. Then write a story about someone using it.

Reflect

How did the form of the clay change from the beginning to the end?

Name ____________________

Foil Figure

MATERIALS

- foil
- scissors
- glue
- cardboard
- scrap paper

Plan

Imagine that you are a statue.
How would you pose?

Create

1. Cut and crumple foil to make a person.

2. Pose your person in different ways. Sketch the actions.

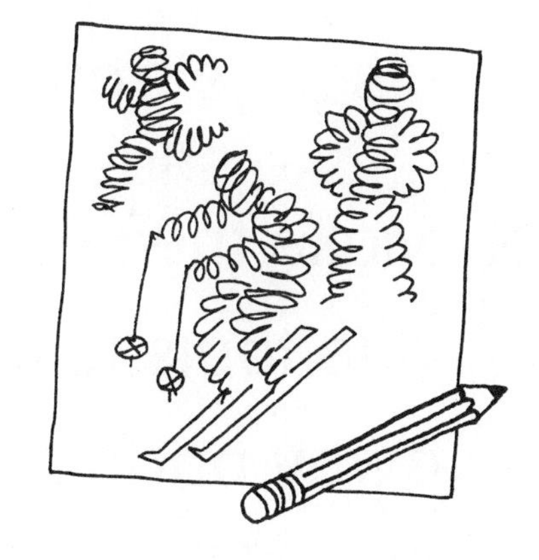

3. Choose your favorite pose and glue. Add details.

4. Write a fact about your person. Then write a letter to him or her.

Reflect

Where do you find space in your sculpture?

Name ______________________________

Timeline Relief Sculpture

MATERIALS
- air-dry clay
- rolling pin
- carving tools
- tempera paints
- paintbrushes

Plan

Think about a time in your life when you learned something special.

Create

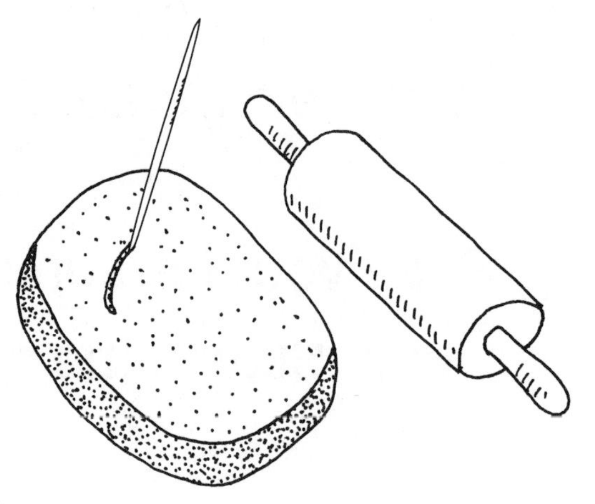

1. Roll out some clay. Draw a scene from your life.
2. Make the scene stand out. Use tools to carve and take away parts of the clay.
3. Paint it when it is dry.
4. Write about how you made the sculpture. Then write the story it shows.

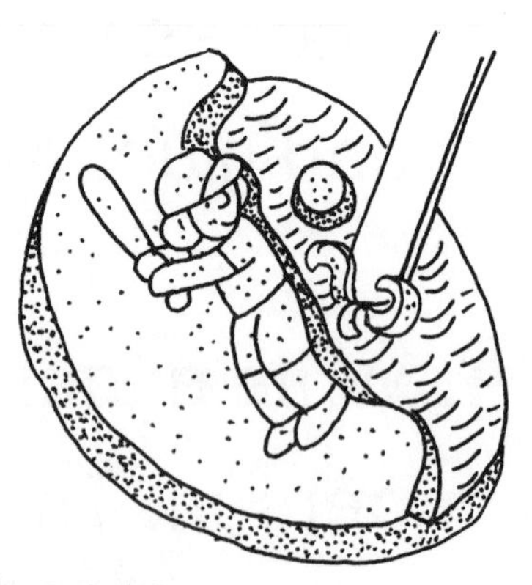

Reflect

What forms did you show?

Name ____________________

Amazing Classroom

MATERIALS

- shoe box
- glue, tape
- paints, brushes
- found materials—thread spools, small milk cartons, wood scraps, paper scraps

Plan

Think about a design for a classroom in an amazing school.

Create

1. Set your box on its side so you can see inside. Make windows.

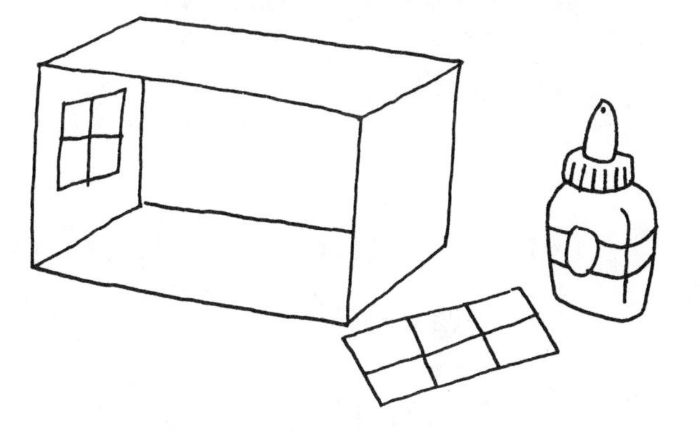

2. Use paper scraps. Paint and glue wallpaper designs inside. Make furniture.

Reflect

What lines, shapes, and forms did you use in your amazing classroom?

3-D Cityscape

MATERIALS
- construction paper
- scissors
- glue
- found objects— yarn, craft sticks, twigs, buttons

Plan

Imagine a city scene with many kinds of buildings.

Create

1. Cut the shape of buildings across the top of a sheet of paper.

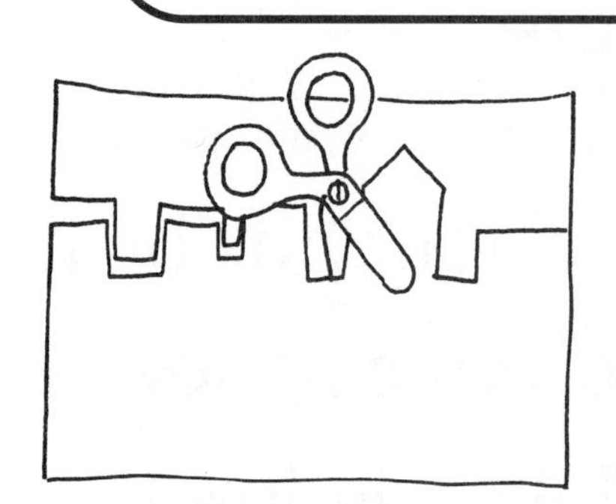

2. Glue it onto another paper.

3. Repeat this to create overlapping. Add details and objects.

Reflect

How does overlapping help show the foreground and background?

Name ________________________________

Night Harbor

MATERIALS

- black construction paper
- oil pastels

Plan

Imagine a nighttime water scene with boats in a harbor.

Create

1. Use black paper. Draw outlines of things found on land and water.

2. Use light colors. Create boats and buildings. Keep a lot of space black.

3. Write a fact about the city. Then imagine that you took a trip to or from this city. Write about it.

Reflect

How did the colors you used make parts of your scene stand out?

Name ______________________________

Paper Sculpture

MATERIALS

- construction paper
- scissors
- glue

Plan

Imagine a sculpture made of paper. Think about the colors and the size.

Create

1. Roll paper into a large cylinder. Glue the edges together.

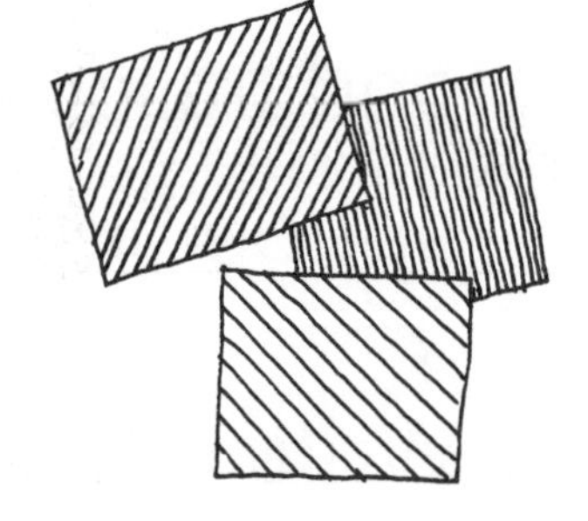

2. Cut paper into small rectangles of different sizes. Roll and glue them to form cylinders.

3. Glue the small cylinders to the large one. Create an interesting sculpture.

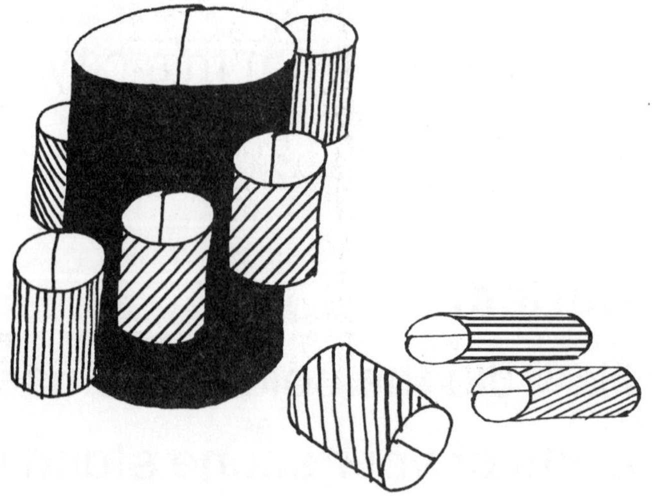

Reflect

What do you see first when you look at your sculpture? Why?

Name ____________________

Tree Design

MATERIALS
- paper
- colored pencils

Plan

Imagine a tree made of shapes. Think about the shapes of the trunk, branches, and leaves.

Create

1. Draw a large tree trunk and branches. Link shapes together as you draw.
2. Add leaves of different shapes. Make the tree balanced.
3. You can add details such as raindrops and clouds.

Reflect

How does your picture show balance? Does it show symmetry?

Name ____________________

Yarn Art

MATERIALS

- construction paper
- many colors of yarn
- glue
- scissors

Plan

Think of a face, object, or design that you could make with yarn.

Create

1. Sketch a picture on paper. Make your picture balanced.

2. Arrange yarn on the picture to create a balance of color. Glue it.

3. Write a display card for your art. Tell the title and how you made it. Then write a story about the art.

Reflect

How did you use colors to give the picture balance?

Paper Hat

MATERIALS

- strips of colored paper, yarn
- stapler
- tape, glue
- found objects—shells, feathers, buttons, seeds

Plan

Think about colors and designs you would like on a hat.

Create

1. Work with a classmate to make a band that fits around your head. Tape it.

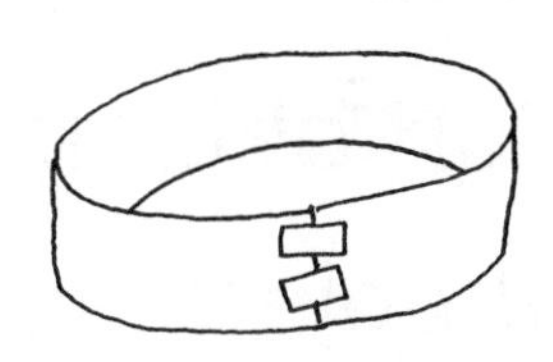

2. Tape some colored strips of paper to the headband to form a hat.

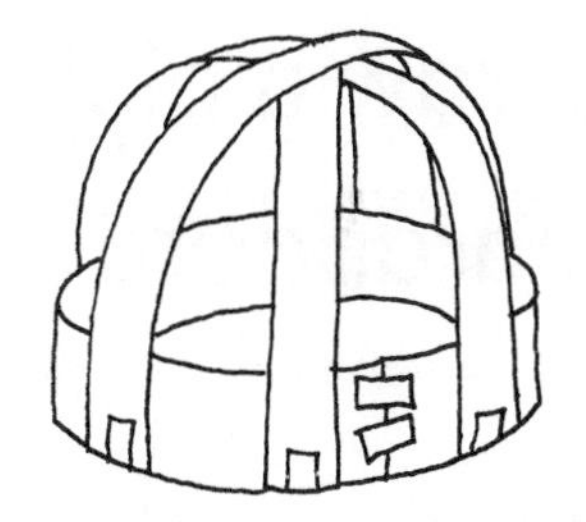

3. Glue on things like feathers or leaves. Weave. Design your hat so that it looks balanced.

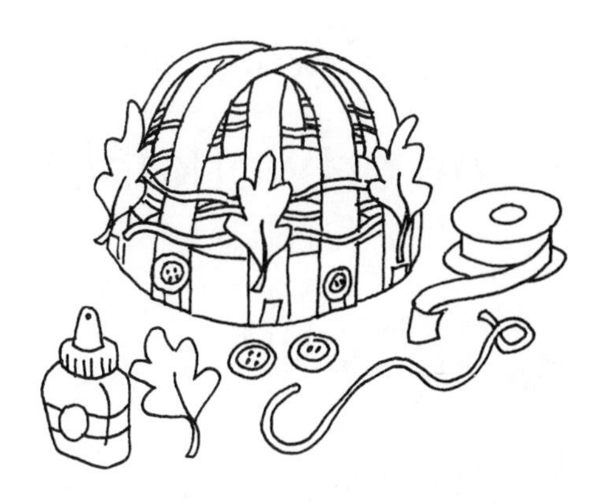

Reflect

How is the design of your hat balanced?
Did you use emphasis? How?

Name ______________________________

Nature Mosaic

MATERIALS

- pebbles, seeds, pieces of bark, other small natural objects
- cardboard
- glue
- pencils or markers

Plan

Think of a picture or design you can make using things like seeds and pebbles.

Create

1. Sort objects from nature by kind of object, color, and size.

2. Draw a picture or design on cardboard.

3. Glue on the objects to make a mosaic. Work to make an artwork that has unity.

Reflect

What did you use to make your mosaic? How does it show unity?

Foil Relief Coin

MATERIALS

- cardboard circles
- foil
- paper scraps, craft sticks, clay
- glue

Plan

Think about a famous person you admire.

Create

1. Draw your famous person on a cardboard coin. Add symbols that show things about the person.

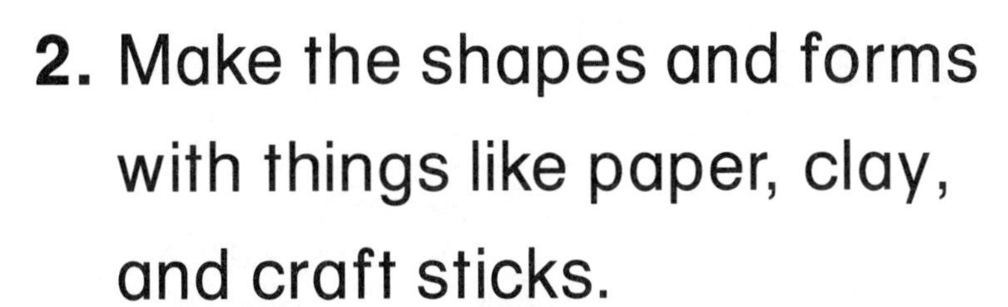

2. Make the shapes and forms with things like paper, clay, and craft sticks.

3. Lay foil over the design. Push down gently.
4. Write a fact about the person. Then write a story about meeting him or her.

Reflect

What do the pictures on your coin stand for?

Sponge-Paint Still Life

MATERIALS

- construction paper
- small pieces of sponge
- tempera paints
- black markers or crayons

Plan

Imagine a vase filled with a variety of flowers.

Create

1. Use sponges to dab paint on the top part of your paper to make a variety of flowers.
2. Add dabs of green where leaves will be.
3. Pull a sponge on the paper to make a vase. Add texture.
4. Use a black marker or crayon to outline flower and leaf shapes. Add details and textures.

Reflect

How did you show variety?

Name ______________________________

Story Cloth

MATERIALS

- heavy cloth with thick weave
- yarn, thread
- scissors
- blunt-tipped needles
- fabric scraps, found objects, craft supplies (buttons, beads)

Plan

Think of a scene from a story or a favorite memory.

Create

1. Sketch the scene on cloth.
2. Cut out pieces of cloth and sew them on. For other parts, stitch the shapes with yarn or thread.

3. Attach things like shells, buttons, and beads. Stitch lines and other details.

Reflect

Tell the story your artwork shows.

Mola Stamp

MATERIALS

- construction paper
- chalk, oil pastels, crayons
- glue
- scissors

Plan

Think of a symbol to show something about your school, city, or state.

Create

1. Many stamps have artwork on them. Your stamp will look like a *mola*. Draw your symbol. Cut it out.
2. Trace around it a little larger on a different color of paper. Cut. Repeat with other colors.

3. Glue the largest shape onto black paper. Glue the other shapes one on top of the other.
4. Add patterns. Add a title.

Reflect

What does your symbol stand for?

Seasonal Activities

Fall

Leaf Prints and Stencils

Materials: leaves, white paper, tempera or watercolor paint, paintbrushes, tape

1. Help children collect some leaves. Have children paint the underside of the leaves and gently press them onto paper to print a design.
2. As a variation, have children use the leaves as stencils. Have them tape their leaves to a sheet of paper. Next, have them use a paintbrush to dab paint around the edges of the leaves. When the paint is dry, remove the leaves.

Wood Sculpture

Materials: wood glue, natural objects: twigs, branches, bark, wood scraps

1. Discuss the various objects that fall from trees such as leaves, pine cones, twigs, and branches. Gather some of these items with children.
2. Have children glue the materials together to form a wood sculpture. Encourage children to use their imagination to create their sculpture. It does not have to resemble a recognizable object—it can be a free-form sculpture.
3. On a classroom table, display a sign labeled *Wood-Sculpture Forest,* and invite children to display their work there.

Patterned Fall Stationery

Materials: computer, word-processing software, paper

1. Have children name some objects that remind them of fall, such as leaves and pumpkins. Tell children that they will use the computer to create fall stationery with seasonal pictures.
2. Demonstrate how to insert clip art pictures into a word-processing document. A procedure like this works: open a new document and select INSERT. Choose Pictures/Clip Art. Show children how to cut and paste pictures to create a pattern around the border of a sheet of paper.
3. Use the fall stationery for classroom correspondence during the season.

Winter

Texture Rubbings

Materials: natural objects, white paper, chalk, crayons

1. Discuss things in nature that have interesting textures, such as pine needles, tree bark, and leaves. Help children collect items like these.
2. Have children place paper over each item and rub the side of chalk or a crayon over it to create a texture rubbing.
3. Suggest that children use their completed rubbing as seasonal gift-wrap or as the background of a homemade holiday card.

Snow Scene

Materials: construction paper, scissors, glue

1. Brainstorm with children a list of things they might see in a snow scene, such as snow figures and snowflakes. Tell children that they will be making a snow scene by combining paper shapes to create new shapes.
2. Have children cut shapes from white paper. Then have them arrange the shapes on dark paper to create a snow scene. Demonstrate how shapes can be joined or overlapped to create new shapes.
3. Display the snow scenes, and invite children to tell how their new shapes were created.

Self-Portrait

Materials: tempera paints, paintbrushes, paper, unbreakable mirrors

1. Tell children that they will be painting a self-portrait. Supply them with mirrors.
2. Encourage children to experiment with mixing neutral colors to create accurate hair colors and skin tones.
3. Make a winter window on a bulletin board to display the portraits. Arrange the faces as if they are looking out the window.

Spring

Spring Color Painting

Materials: paper, watercolor paints, paintbrushes

1. Ask children what colors come to mind when they think about springtime. Tell them that they will be using the dry-brush technique to fill a page with spring colors.
2. Dampen the watercolor paints and demonstrate how to make sweeping strokes of color across a dry sheet of paper. Encourage children to use their imagination to create their spring color painting.
3. Display the paintings on a bulletin board entitled "Colors of Spring".

Papier-Mâché Flowerpot

Materials: small empty milk cartons, newspaper, glue, bowls, tempera paint, scissors, construction paper, chenille sticks, crayons

1. Tell children they are going to make a papier-mâché flowerpot.
2. Mix water and glue in bowls and distribute them to children. Give each child an empty milk carton. Have them open the carton completely and cover the outside with strips of newspaper dipped in the glue mixture.
3. Have children draw, color, and cut out flowers to attach to chenille sticks to put into their flowerpots.
4. After the papier-mâché dries, have children paint and decorate their flowerpots.

Spring Hat

Materials: glue, scissors, newspaper, found materials such as paper scraps, old buttons, cloth scraps, pieces of string and yarn

1. Tell children that they will be making a spring hat out of recycled materials.
2. Guide children in folding a newspaper to form a hat. Have children cut spring flowers, birds, and plants from the found materials and glue them onto their hat.
3. Have a parade. Play music and invite children to wear their hats while moving and marching to the music.

Seasonal Activities

Summer

Stitching a Design

Materials: large-eyed plastic children's needles, yarn and thread, coarse cloth, scissors

1. Ask children to name some items that remind them of summer, such as sunshine and the beach. Tell children that they will use colored thread to stitch a summer design.
2. Distribute pieces of coarse cloth and sewing supplies. Help children to thread their needles and then to sew safely. Have children sketch the design they would like to stitch before they begin.
3. Invite children to show their completed design to the group and tell about it.

Summertime Fruit Bowl

Materials: salt dough, food coloring

1. Ask children to name some of the fruits that they eat in the summer, such as watermelon, apples, and berries. Tell children that they will use salt dough to make some fruit.
2. Distribute salt dough and food coloring. Guide children to add food coloring to the dough, mixing colors to get the colors they want.
3. Have children form fruit from the dough. After the fruit is dry, display it in a basket.

Make Nature Paper

Materials: blender, scrap paper, framed section of screen, dishpan, cloths or dish towels, newspaper, rolling pin, natural objects: petals, leaves, seeds, optional: iron, starch

1. Help children put small pieces of scrap paper into a blender with water to make pulp. Pour it into a dishpan.
2. Have children dip a section of screen into the pulp and raise it up, making a thin, even layer. Cover it with a cloth and gently push to drain the water. Then children can gently push things like petals and seeds into the layer.
3. Cover the layer with a dry cloth, turn it over onto newspaper, and put another cloth on top. Have children use a rolling pin to remove more water. You can also use an iron to dry the paper. Then gently pull on either side of the cloths to loosen the paper.
4. To make the paper better for writing on, spray with starch, cover with a cloth, and iron.

School–Home Connection

Dear Family Member,

Your child is learning about lines and shapes in art and in the environment, and is making art that uses these elements of art. The unit theme is "Celebrate Our World."

Here are vocabulary and concepts your child will be learning about in this unit.

lines
outline
movement
geometric shapes
free-form shapes
organic shapes
portrait
self-portrait

Try This!

At the Library

Share a picture book with your child that shows clear lines and shapes, such as books by Dr. Seuss or Lois Ehlert. Talk with your child about the kinds of lines and shapes he or she sees in the art.

Sketchbook

Encourage your child to sketch the lines and shapes of things he or she observes indoors, such as furniture, and outdoors, such as trees and leaves. Help your child write labels for information he or she wants to record.

Art Puzzlers

- Draw in the air the **lines** that lightning makes. Tell about the lines.
- Look around. Which things have lines that show **movement**?
- Use your finger to trace an **outline** around your shoe and then around your hand.
- Look at clothing. Look outside. Find **geometric, free-form,** and **organic shapes.**
- What **geometric shape** is pizza? Name some other foods that have geometric shapes.

La escuela y la casa

Estimado miembro de la familia:

Su hijo está aprendiendo sobre las líneas y las figuras en el arte y su alrededor. Además está produciendo arte que utiliza esos mismos elementos. El tema de la unidad es "La celebración de nuestro mundo".

Éstas son las palabras del vocabulario y los conceptos de esta unidad que su hijo estará aprendiendo.

líneas
contorno
movimiento
figuras geométricas
figuras de forma libre
figuras orgánicas
retrato
autorretrato

¡Inténtalo!

En la biblioteca

Comparta con su hijo un libro con ilustraciones de líneas y figuras, como los libros escritos por Dr. Seuss o Lois Ehlert. Luego, hablen sobre las diferentes líneas y figuras que ven en cada ilustración.

Libro de dibujo

Anime a su hijo a dibujar las líneas y figuras de cosas que observa adentro o afuera de la casa, como por ejemplo muebles, árboles u hojas. Ayúdele a escribir toda la información que sea necesaria.

Acertijos de arte

- Dibuja en el aire las **líneas** que forman los rayos de una tormenta.
- Mira a tu alrededor. ¿Qué cosas tienen líneas que muestran **movimiento**?
- Usa el dedo para trazar el **contorno** de tu zapato y de tu mano.
- Mira tu ropa. Mira afuera. Busca **figuras geométricas, figuras de forma libre** y **figuras orgánicas**.
- ¿Qué **figura geométrica** tiene una pizza? Nombra otras comidas que tengan figuras geométricas.

School-Home Connection

Dear Family Member,

Your child is learning about color and value in art and in the environment, and is making art that uses these elements of art. The unit theme is "Mix and Match."

Here are vocabulary and concepts your child will be learning about in this unit.

primary colors	**tint**
secondary colors	**shade**
warm colors	**mood**
cool colors	**seascape**
value	**horizon line**

Try This!

At the Library

Share a colorful picture book with your child such as books by Eric Carle or Gerald McDermott. Talk with your child about the colors and moods in the art.

On the Go

When you drive or walk with your child, talk about the colors of buildings, signs, flowers, and cars. Ask your child if the colors are warm or cool, light or dark. Also, ask how the colors make him or her feel.

Art Puzzlers

- Name the **colors** of some fruits and vegetables.
- How do you feel? What **colors** describe your **mood**?
- Look around. Point to light **colors** and **dark colors**.
- What **colors** would be in a **story** that is loud and full of action? In a story that is quiet and still?
- Name things you might see in a **seascape**, such as the color blue.

La escuela y la casa

Estimado miembro de la familia:

Su hijo está aprendiendo sobre los colores y el valor en el arte y su alrededor. Además está produciendo arte que utiliza esos mismos elementos. El tema de la unidad es “Mezcla de colores”.

Éstas son las palabras del vocabulario y los conceptos de esta unidad que su hijo estará aprendiendo.

colores primarios	**tinte**
colores secundarios	**matiz**
colores cálidos	**sentir**
colores fríos	**vista marina**
valor	**línea del horizonte**

¡Inténtalo!

En la biblioteca

Comparta con su hijo un libro con dibujos llenos de colores como los libros de Eric Carle o Gerald McDermott. Hable con su hijo sobre los diferentes colores y el sentir que inspira una obra de arte.

En camino

Mientras camine o vaya en el auto con su hijo, señale los colores de los edificios, los letreros, las flores y los autos. Pregunte a su hijo si los colores son cálidos o fríos, claros u oscuros. Pregúntele también cómo se siente al ver esos colores.

Acertijos de arte

- Nombra los **colores** de algunas frutas y verduras.
- ¿Cómo te sientes? ¿Cuáles **colores** describen tu **sentir**?
- Mira a tu alrededor. Señala los **colores claros.** Señala los **colores oscuros.**
- ¿Cuáles **colores** estarían en un **cuento** lleno de acción? ¿En un cuento tranquilo?
- Nombra algunas cosas que verías en una **vista marina**, como por ejemplo el color azul.

School-Home Connection

Dear Family Member,

Your child is learning about patterns, rhythms, and textures in art and in the environment, and is making art that uses these elements and principles. The unit theme is "Nature's Way."

Here are vocabulary and concepts your child will be learning about in this unit.

pattern
repetition
print
rhythm
texture
weaving
visual texture

Try This!

Pattern Game

Describe a pattern to your child, and have him or her finish it. For example, say *red, red, blue; red, red, blue*. Ask your child to continue the pattern. Make up more patterns together.

Explore Textures

Ask your child to close his or her eyes. Place an object with a rough or other interesting texture in his or her hands. Ask your child to describe the texture and then guess what the object is.

Art Puzzlers

- Name something with a bumpy **texture.** Name something with a soft texture.
- Continue this **shape pattern:** square-square-circle-triangle, square-square-circle-triangle.
- Look outside. Tell what repeating colors, lines, and shapes create a **rhythm** that your eyes follow.
- Arrange some crayons in a **color pattern.** Tell what you did.
- Look at the **designs** in clothing around you. What **patterns** of lines and shapes do you see repeated?

La escuela y la casa

Estimado miembro de la familia:

Su hijo está aprendiendo sobre los patrones, los ritmos y las texturas en el arte y su alrededor. Además está produciendo arte que utiliza esos mismos elementos. El tema de la unidad es "La naturaleza".

Éstas son las palabras del vocabulario y los conceptos de esta unidad que su hijo estará aprendiendo.

patrón
repetición
grabado
ritmo
textura
tejido
textura visual

¡Inténtalo!

Juego de patrones

Describa un patrón a su hijo y pídale que lo termine. Por ejemplo, diga *rojo, rojo, azul; rojo, rojo, azul*. Después diga a su hijo que continue el patrón.

Explorar texturas

Pida a su hijo que cierre los ojos. Coloque en sus manos un objeto con una textura áspera. Pídale que describa la textura y después que trate de identificar el objeto.

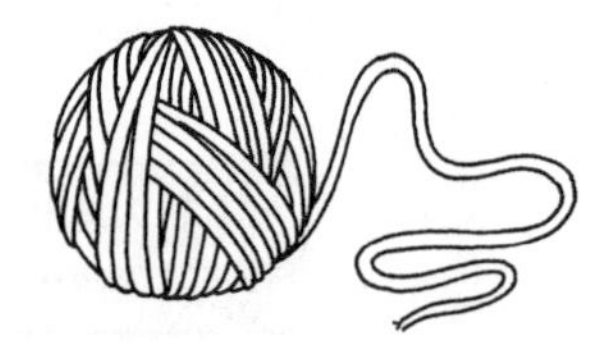

Acertijos de arte

- Nombra algo con una **textura** áspera. Nombra algo con una textura suave.
- Continua este **patrón de figuras**: cuadro-cuadro-círculo-triángulo, cuadro-cuadro-círculo-triángulo.
- Mira hacia afuera. Di cuáles colores, líneas y figuras repetidas crean un **ritmo** que siguen tus ojos.
- Arregla algunos crayones en un **patrón de colores**. Explica lo que hiciste.
- Mira los **diseños** en la ropa de tu alrededor. ¿Qué **patrones** de líneas y figuras repetidos ves?

School-Home Connection

Dear Family Member,

Your child is learning about form and space in art and in the environment, and is making art that uses these elements of art. The unit theme is "Surprises Everywhere."

Here are vocabulary and concepts your child will be learning about in this unit.

form
sculpture
space
relief sculpture
architecture
architect
landscape
foreground
background

Try This!

Look at Buildings

When you go places with your child, talk about different kinds of buildings you see. Ask your child to describe shapes, forms, and patterns he or she notices. Compare the architecture of two buildings.

Sketchbook

Encourage your child to sketch the foreground and the background in a particular room or outdoor setting.

Art Puzzlers

- Find a **form** that is like a **sphere.** Find one like a **cube.**
- Imagine you are in a toy store. What do you see in the **foreground**? What do you see in the **background**?
- If you were an **architect**, describe how you would use **forms**, **shapes**, and **space.**
- What do you see in a winter **landscape**? A spring **landscape**?
- What **forms** do you see that have **space** to walk all around them?

La escuela y la casa

Estimado miembro de la familia:

Su hijo está aprendiendo sobre la forma y el espacio en el arte y su alrededor. Además está produciendo arte que utiliza esos mismos elementos. El tema de la unidad es "Sorpresas por todas partes".

Éstas son las palabras del vocabulario y los conceptos de esta unidad que su hijo estará aprendiendo.

forma
escultura
espacio
escultura en relieve
arquitectura
arquitecto
paisaje
primer plano
fondo

¡Inténtalo!

Ver edificios

Cuando salga con su hijo, señale diferentes edificios. Pida a su hijo que describa los detalles de la arquitectura, tales coma las figuras, las formas y los patrones. Comparen la arquitectura de varios edificios.

Libro de dibujo

Anime a su hijo a dibujar el primer plano y el fondo de un cuarto o de un lugar de afuera.

Acertijos de arte

- Busca una **forma** que se parezca a una **esfera.** Busca una que se parezca a un **cubo.**
- Imagina que estás en una juguetería. ¿Qué ves en el **primer plano**? ¿Qué ves en el **fondo**?
- Si fueras **arquitecto**, describe cómo usarías las **formas**, las **figuras** y el **espacio.**
- ¿Qué ves en un **paisaje** del invierno? ¿Y en un **paisaje** de la primavera?
- ¿Cuáles **formas** ves que tienen **espacio** para caminar a su alrededor?

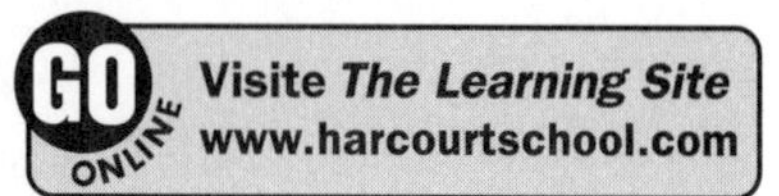

School-Home Connection

Dear Family Member,

Your child is learning about emphasis and balance in art and in the environment, and is making art that uses these principles of design. The unit theme is "Good Neighbors."

Here are vocabulary and concepts your child will be learning about in this unit.

emphasis
subject
balance
symmetry
contrast
textiles
designs

Try This!

At the Library

Page through a picture book with your child, focusing on the artwork. On several pages, pause and ask your child to point to the things in each picture that stand out the most, or have the greatest emphasis. Talk about why.

Partner Drawing

Fold a sheet of paper in half. Work with your child to create a picture that has balance. Draw a shape on one side of the paper and have your child draw the same thing on the other. Continue adding shapes and simple pictures until you have created a balanced picture you like.

Art Puzzlers

- What things on both sides of your face and your body give it **balance**?
- Point to an object that has **symmetry**. Use your finger to trace an imaginary line down the middle of the object.
- Look around. Tell what object you notice first. What gives it **emphasis**—its color or its size?
- Arrange objects to show **balance.** Tell what you did and why.
- Look at the art on a book cover or a poster. What is the **subject**?

Visit *The Learning Site*
www.harcourtschool.com

La escuela y la casa

Estimado miembro de la familia:

Su hijo está aprendiendo sobre el énfasis y el equilibrio en el arte y su alrededor. Además está produciendo arte que utiliza esos mismos elementos de diseño. El tema de la unidad es "Buenos vecinos".

Éstas son las palabras del vocabulario y los conceptos de esta unidad que su hijo estará aprendiendo.

énfasis
tema
equilibrio
simetría
contraste
textiles
diseños

¡Inténtalo!

En la biblioteca

Comparta un libro de ilustraciones con su hijo enfocándose en los dibujos. En cada página, haga una pausa y pida a su hijo que identifique las cosas que se destaquen o que tengan el mayor énfasis. Hablen sobre sus observaciones.

Dibujar en pareja

Trabaje con su hijo para crear un dibujo con equilibrio. Doble una hoja a la mitad. Dibuje una figura en un lado de la hoja y diga a su hijo que dibuje lo mismo en el otro lado. Sigan añadiendo figuras y dibujos sencillos hasta que estén satisfechos con el dibujo final.

Acertijos de arte

- ¿Qué cosas dan **equilibrio** en ambos lados de tu cara y de tu cuerpo?
- Señala un objeto con **simetría**. Traza una línea imaginaria por el centro del objeto con tu dedo.
- Mira a tu alrededor. Nombra el objeto que ves primero. ¿Qué le da **énfasis**, su color o su tamaño?
- Arregla algunos objetos para mostrar **equilibrio**. Explica lo que hiciste y por qué.
- Mira la cubierta de un libro de arte o un cartel. ¿Cuál es el **tema**?

School-Home Connection

Dear Family Member,

Your child is learning about unity and variety in art and in the environment, and is making art that uses these principles of design. The unit theme is "World Treasures."

Here are vocabulary and concepts your child will be learning about in this unit.

mosaic
unity
symbol
still life
variety
story cloth
graphic art

Try This!

Collage

Page through old magazines with your child. Find pictures of things that look like they belong together and cut them out. Write *Unity* in the center of a sheet of paper. Arrange the pictures around the word, and glue them to form a collage.

Sketchbook

Gather foods from the kitchen, such as fruits, vegetables, and canned goods. Help your child place them in an interesting still life arrangement. Have your child sketch the still life in his or her sketchbook.

Art Puzzlers

- A tree with leaves has **unity.** All parts look like they belong together. Name other things in nature that show unity.
- Describe a meal with a **variety** of food and a toy store with a variety of toys.
- What **symbol** on your paper means "good work"? What are symbols for our country? For sports teams?
- Describe **graphic art** you have seen on food packages, such as cereal boxes and fruit juices.
- Place things on a table to show **variety.** Arrange them to be an interesting **still life.**

GO ONLINE Visit *The Learning Site* www.harcourtschool.com

La escuela y la casa

Estimado miembro de la familia:

Su hijo está aprendiendo sobre la unidad y la variedad en el arte y su alrededor. Además está produciendo arte que utiliza esos mismos elementos. El tema de la unidad es "Los tesoros del mundo".

Éstas son las palabras del vocabulario y los conceptos de esta unidad que su hijo estará aprendiendo.

mosaico
unidad
símbolo
bodegón
variedad
tapiz histórico
arte gráfico

¡Inténtalo!

Collage

Comparta revistas viejas con su hijo. Busquen y recorten algunas ilustraciones de cosas que representen unidad. Escriban *Unidad* en el centro de una hoja. Arreglen las ilustraciones alrededor de la palabra y péguenlas para formar un collage.

Libro de dibujo

Junte comida de la cocina como frutas, verduras y comida enlatada. Ayude a su hijo a arreglarlas en un bodegón interesante. Pídale que dibuje el bodegón en su libro de dibujos.

Acertijos de arte

- Un árbol con hojas muestra la **unidad**. Nombra otras cosas en la naturaleza que muestren **unidad**.
- Describe una comida con una **variedad** de alimentos y una juguetería con una variedad de juguetes.
- ¿Cuál **símbolo** en tu hoja representa "buen trabajo"? ¿Cuáles son los símbolos de nuestro país? ¿Y los de equipos deportivos?
- Describe el **arte gráfico** que has visto en paquetes de comida.
- Coloca diferentes objetos en una mesa para mostrar **variedad** y arréglalas en un **bodegón** interesante.

GO ONLINE Visite *The Learning Site* www.harcourtschool.com

Unit Tests

Directions

These Unit Tests are a combination of multiple-choice and constructed response questions that allow children to summarize and apply what they have learned in each unit. Some questions assess learning through drawing tasks.

A Unit Test may be administered orally, or the page may be duplicated and distributed to each child. When children have finished, discuss the answers, allowing them the opportunity to reflect on their responses and to explain their knowledge. Accept reasonable answers for the constructed response questions.

The following rubric may be used in scoring the drawing response items. Score as correct the responses receiving scores of 3 or 2, and score as incorrect the responses receiving scores of 1 or 0.

Score of 3	The response shows understanding, good attention to detail, and imagination. The response is neat and shows good effort.
Score of 2	The response shows understanding and some attention to detail. The response could show more imagination and more effort, but is still successful.
Score of 1	The response shows little or no understanding or attention to detail. The response shows little imagination and minimal effort.
Score of 0	There is no response or the response is not related. There is no attention to detail and shows minimal use of imagination. The response shows limited effort.

Read each question aloud to children to ensure their understanding of the task.

Answer Key

Best responses are shown. (Parentheses show examples of possible answers; however, accept other reasonable responses.)

Unit 1

1 B
2 C
3 A
4 C
5 B
6 (child's name, myself)
7–9 (drawing of a geometric shape—circle, triangle, square, rectangle, or oval)
10 (free-form drawing of shape from nature—leaf, flower, etc.)

Unit 2

1 A
2 D
3 C
4 B
5 D
6 B
7 (red, blue, or yellow)
8 (blue, purple, or green)
9 (warm)
10 (drawing with a horizontal line separating earth and sky)

Unit 3

1 B
2 C
3 B
4 A
5 D
6 C
7 D
8 C
9 (Possible responses: bumpy, smooth)
10 (pattern of shapes)

Unit 4

1 A
2 D
3 B
4 C
5 A
6 B
7 B
8 (something from outdoors)
9 (circle around the tree)
10 (X on the house)

Unit 5

1 C
2 B
3 D
4 B
5 A
6 C
7 C (or D)
8 B
9 (child riding a bike)
10 (drawing that is the same on both sides)

Unit 6

1 C
2 C
3 B
4 D
5 A
6 C
7 B
8 C
9 (Possible response: a handshake)
10 (unified drawing with a variety of things)

Name ______________________ Date ____________ **Unit 1 Test**

1 An ________ is the line along the edge of a shape.

Ⓐ portrait Ⓒ zigzag
Ⓑ outline Ⓓ curved

2 Lines that curve and bend through an artwork can show ________.

Ⓐ form Ⓒ movement
Ⓑ portrait Ⓓ tints

3 Thin, curved, and horizontal are kinds of ________.

Ⓐ lines Ⓒ shapes
Ⓑ circles Ⓓ landscape

4 Organic shapes can also be called ________ shapes.

Ⓐ balance Ⓒ free-form
Ⓑ architecture Ⓓ geometric

5 Which of the following is a portrait?

Ⓐ

Ⓑ

Ⓒ

Ⓓ

6 Who would you paint in a self-portrait? ____________________

7–9 Draw a different geometric shape in each box.

7 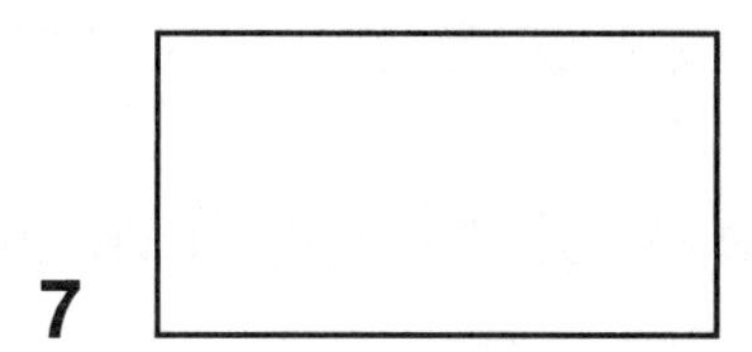

8 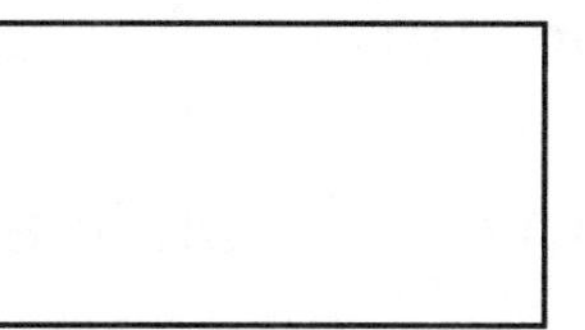

9 

10 Draw a picture of an organic shape on the back of your paper.

Name ______________________ Date ____________ **Unit 2 Test**

1 The feeling colors can give is called ________.

Ⓐ mood
Ⓑ free-form
Ⓒ self-portrait
Ⓓ outline

2 Make a ________ by mixing a color with black.

Ⓐ tint
Ⓑ jewelry
Ⓒ variety
Ⓓ shade

3 Make a ________ by mixing a color with white.

Ⓐ shade
Ⓑ photograph
Ⓒ tint
Ⓓ shape

4 The lightness or darkness of a color is called its ________.

Ⓐ geometric shape
Ⓑ value
Ⓒ mood
Ⓓ organic shape

5 When primary colors are mixed, they make ________.

Ⓐ shades
Ⓑ shapes
Ⓒ horizon lines
Ⓓ secondary colors

6 You would most likely see ________ in a seascape.

Ⓐ a city
Ⓑ the ocean
Ⓒ a room
Ⓓ a forest

7 One primary color is ____________________.

8 One cool color is ____________________.

9 Red and orange are both ____________________ colors.

10 Draw a picture with a horizon line on the back of your paper.

Name ______________________________ Date ____________ **Unit 3 Test**

1 The way something feels is its ________.

Ⓐ zigzag
Ⓑ texture
Ⓒ movement
Ⓓ color wheel

2 Texture we can see but not touch is ________.

Ⓐ mood
Ⓑ self-portrait
Ⓒ visual texture
Ⓓ movement

3 An artwork that is a copy, made by pressing paint onto paper with an object, is called a ________.

Ⓐ balance
Ⓑ print
Ⓒ line
Ⓓ outline

4 A ________ is an artwork made by putting materials over and under each other.

Ⓐ weaving
Ⓑ portrait
Ⓒ self-portrait
Ⓓ landscape

5 The movement that comes from patterns is ________.

Ⓐ outline
Ⓑ geometric
Ⓒ warm color
Ⓓ rhythm

6 ________ is used to make patterns.

Ⓐ Mood
Ⓑ Primary color
Ⓒ Repetition
Ⓓ Cool color

7 Artists add texture to pictures with lines and ________.

Ⓐ portraits Ⓑ moods Ⓒ value Ⓓ colors

8 Lines, shapes, and colors that repeat are called ________.

Ⓐ moods Ⓑ outlines Ⓒ patterns Ⓓ seascapes

9 Write a word that names a kind of texture. ______________

10 Draw a pattern of shapes on the back of your paper.

Name ______________________ Date ____________ **Unit 4 Test**

1 The art and science of planning buildings is ________.

Ⓐ architecture Ⓒ landscape
Ⓑ organic shape Ⓓ movement

2 An architect would create a ________.

Ⓐ painting Ⓑ statue Ⓒ photograph Ⓓ house

3 An artwork you can see from all sides is a ________.

Ⓐ photograph Ⓑ sculpture Ⓒ portrait Ⓓ shade

4 An artwork with height, width, and depth has ________.

Ⓐ balance Ⓑ outline Ⓒ form Ⓓ horizon line

5 The part of an artwork that is not filled in is ________.

Ⓐ space Ⓒ architecture
Ⓑ geometric shape Ⓓ line

6 A sculpture carved on a flat surface is a ________.

Ⓐ weaving Ⓒ seascape
Ⓑ relief sculpture Ⓓ shape

7 Which of these is a sculpture?

Ⓐ a painting Ⓒ a photograph
Ⓑ a statue Ⓓ a house

8 Name an object you would see in a landscape. ______________

9 Circle the object in the foreground of this picture.

10 Put an ✗ on the object in the background.

Name ______________________ Date ____________ **Unit 5 Test**

1 Pictures and patterns in artworks are ________.

Ⓐ portraits Ⓑ tints Ⓒ designs Ⓓ architect

2 Artists use light and dark colors to show ________.

Ⓐ symmetry Ⓑ contrast Ⓒ color wheel Ⓓ form

3 The use of color to make things stand out is called ________.

Ⓐ balance Ⓒ architecture
Ⓑ weaving Ⓓ emphasis

4 An artwork has ________ if both sides are the same.

Ⓐ shape Ⓑ symmetry Ⓒ mood Ⓓ variety

5 Another word for cloth and fabric is ________.

Ⓐ textiles Ⓒ print
Ⓑ free-form Ⓓ architecture

6 Artists use ________ to make parts seem equal.

Ⓐ emphasis Ⓒ balance
Ⓑ movement Ⓓ outline

7 Which picture below best shows balance? ________

8 Which picture below best shows contrast? ________

9 What is the subject of Picture C? ____________________

A 
B 
C 
D 

10 Draw a picture that has symmetry on the back of your paper.

Name ______________________ Date ____________ **Unit 6 Test**

1 An artwork with many different things in it has ________.

Ⓐ symmetry Ⓑ mood Ⓒ variety Ⓓ form

2 An artwork made from textiles that tells a story is a ________.

Ⓐ statue Ⓑ movement Ⓒ story cloth Ⓓ photograph

3 A thing that stands for an important idea is a ________.

Ⓐ print Ⓑ symbol Ⓒ shape Ⓓ balance

4 An artwork made with small pieces of paper, tile, glass, or stone is a ________.

Ⓐ self-portrait Ⓑ painting Ⓒ contrast Ⓓ mosaic

5 When all the parts belong or work together, the artwork has ________.

Ⓐ unity Ⓑ mood Ⓒ form Ⓓ weaving

6 The art in magazines and on cereal boxes is ________.

Ⓐ landscape art Ⓒ graphic art
Ⓑ mosaic art Ⓓ variety

7 A ________ is a picture of objects that are grouped together.

Ⓐ movement Ⓒ zigzag
Ⓑ still-life Ⓓ color wheel

8 Which of the following is a still life?

A  B  C  D 

9 A symbol for friendship could be ______________________.

10 Draw a picture that shows variety on the back of your paper.